A Sense of Order

THE RURAL LANDSCAPE OF LOWER PUTAH CREEK

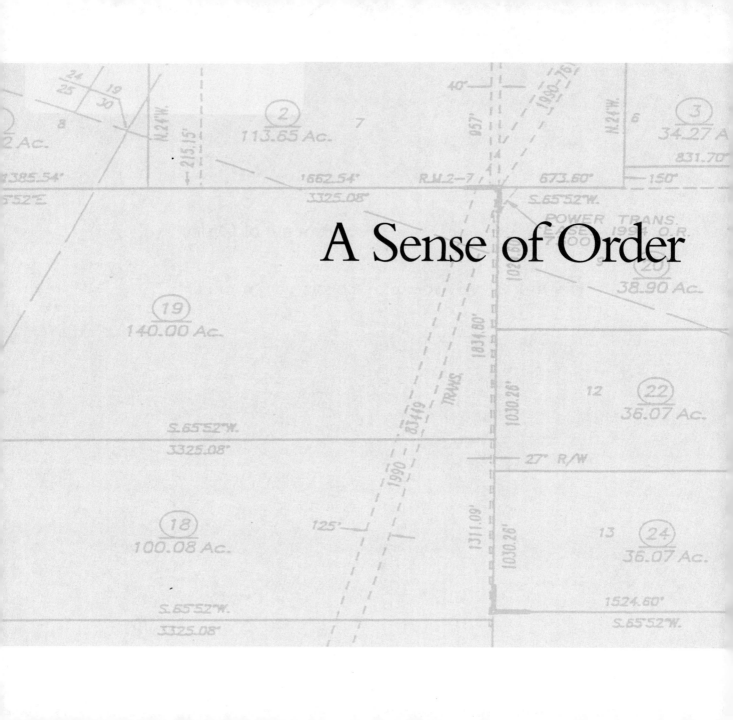

A Sense of Order

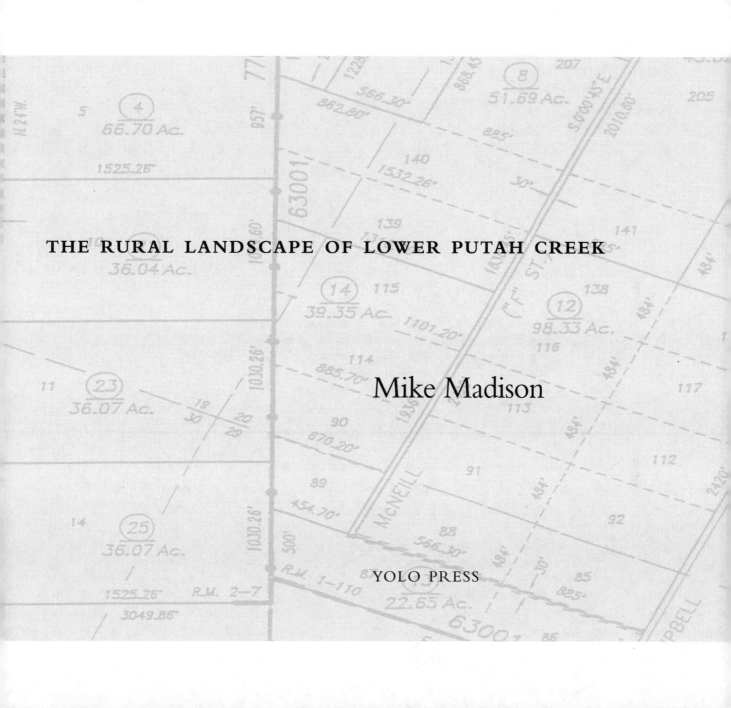

THE RURAL LANDSCAPE OF LOWER PUTAH CREEK

Mike Madison

YOLO PRESS

Mike Madison
Yolo Press
Copyright© 2002 by Mike Madison

All rights reserved. No part of this book may be reproduced or transmitted in any form or by any means, electronic, photographic, or mechanical, without permission in writing from the publisher. Individuals and not-for-profit organizations may photocopy this work for their own use. For information, contact the publisher:

Yolo Press, 6446 Putah Creek Lane, Winters, California, 95694.

Portions of this work appeared in an essay titled 'A Place in the Country' in the journal *Environs*, Spring 2002.

ISBN 0-9662908-2-8

Printed in the United States of America by
Gorham Printing, Rochester, WA

Book design by Kathryn E. Campbell

ACKNOWLEDGEMENTS

This work was prepared under the aegis of the Putah-Cache Bioregion Project of the University of California at Davis. I wish to thank the director of the bioregion project, David Robertson, for his friendship and support. My colleagues in the project—Julia Levine, Laurie Glover, Maria Melendez, Dan Leroy, Sarah Motley, Janet Riehl, Fran Ransley, Amy Boyer, Kelly Lyons, and Jamie Chomas—have been stimulating companions. I have gathered much useful information from local residents, including Bobby Borchard, Bill Schroeder, John Rotteveel, Dave Scheuring, Craig McNamara, Joann Larkey, David Viguie, Ramon Cadena, and Paul Lum. I am particularly indebted to Jack Phillips for sharing his wide knowledge, impeccable memory, and wry sense of humor. The staff of Shields Library were unfailingly helpful. I am grateful to Robert Milbrodt of the Yolo County Assessor's Office for providing the parcel map used in Figure 6, and to Jamie Madison for configuring the graph in Figure 7.

6 A SENSE OF ORDER

CONTENTS

1. Reading the landscape / 9
2. Earth / 15
3. Water / 25
4. Air / 31
5. Fire / 37
6. Vegetation / 41
7. Agriculture / 51
8. Machines / 83
9. Rural structures / 93
10. Town / 115
11. Wealth is theft / 129
12. The Experience of Landscape / 139

Figure 1. Rural scene with standpipe. Solano County

Chapter One:

Reading the Landscape

> There is good reading on the land, first-hand reading, involving no symbols.
>
> Mae Theigaard Watts,
> *Reading the Landscape*, 1957

> A rich and beautiful book is always open before us. We have but to learn to read it.
>
> J.B. Jackson,
> *The Need for Being Versed in Country Things*, 1951

> The eye may be less reliable than the mind, or even the heart.
>
> Anthony D. King,
> *The Politics of Vision,* 1997

> Ordinary landscape seems messy and disorganized, like a book with pages missing, torn and smudged; a book whose copy has been edited and re-edited by people with illegible handwriting. Like books, landscapes can be read, but unlike books, they were not meant to be read.
>
> Pierce F. Lewis,
> *Axioms for Reading the Landscape*, 1979

IMAGE AND TEXT

Walking through open country in the lower Sacramento Valley, stop, and look to the west. In the foreground is a field of copper-colored safflower, beyond that an apple-green field of sudan grass, then the irregular dark green stripe of an almond orchard, in the far distance mountains of a hazy indigo, and above that a cloudless sky. The word 'landscape' could refer to the actual, physical place, or to a recorded image of it, such as a photograph or a painting. In either case, the subject is an outdoor scene characterized by a generosity of space and a depth of view.

Consider the landscape depicted in figure one. It is a typical rural scene of the region, with flat land planted to crops, and distant mountains. In the foreground is a standpipe, a vertical concrete cylinder that serves to vent an underground pipeline of irrigation water. To a landscape painter, having set up her easel before this prospect, the scene is one of horizontality; the fields and orchards appear as a stack of thin horizontal lines—umber, green, golden—and above them the purplish line of mountains. The standpipe is a vertical element in this composition. The painter might choose to delete it from her canvas, or she might relocate it on the canvas to a different spot where it better serves her, or she might make a row of standpipes disappearing into the distance to establish perspective or direct the viewer's eye. She might choose to emphasize the blueness of the shadow cast by the white pipe, or the red aura at the edge of that shadow. Often the most truthful image is not a literal one, and hewing closer to the truth by departing from the literal is the realm in which the landscape painter's genius operates. Whatever her treatment of it, the artist deals with the standpipe purely in the realm of image.

But to another viewer, surveying the scene from the same spot, the standpipe is an element of text. Meaning can be drawn from it, or projected onto it. As text, the landscape is the image labeled, annotated, captioned, verbalized; its features are symbolic as well as visual. To a hydraulic engineer, the standpipe is a sign that something interesting is going on with the pipeline under ground—either a branching, or a valve, or a sharp turn—for which the standpipe serves to relieve the pressure wave that develops in such spots. To a wildlife biologist, the standpipe indicates water stolen from a stream to the detriment of the natural stream habitat and its animals. A banker sees the standpipe and mentally adds two hundred dollars per acre to the value of the land, because it is supplied with cheap district water. For a political scientist the standpipe triggers a suite of reflections on the importance of a strong central government in establishing a regional hydraulic system. The economist muses on the amortization of public investment, and how it plays itself out in fortunes public and private. To a social activist, the standpipe symbolizes how the mainstream farmers monopolize the main stream of water, and how the marginal farmers—marginal socially and marginal geographically—must farm the dry lands away from the main stream.

A thoughtful and well-informed viewer may read all of these texts from the image simultaneously, and perhaps others as well. And then there will be some who look at the scene and see only a concrete pipe, mute and textless, unconnected to any thought. Like mathematics, a system of landscape symbols needs the concept of zero.

So in addition to being an image, a landscape is a collection of texts. There is an economic landscape, a historical landscape, an ecological landscape, a political landscape, a hydraulic landscape, an ethical landscape, and many others. Each of these disciplines has its own language, its own grammar and syntax, rhetoric and poetics. Reading a landscape in conflicting languages is a source of strife in land use and zoning discussions; the conservationist who sees a vernal pool as a vital habitat is not reading the same text as the developer who sees is it as a spot propitious for a warehouse. Whether there is a universal language of landscape, and if there is, whether it is sufficiently articulated to be of any use, is still unclear. What is clear, as Lewis Pierce observes in a remark quoted at the top of the chapter, is that landscapes can be read, but they are not meant to be read.

Figure 2. The landscape of horizontal lines: melons, squash, wheat, corn, trees, sky. Yolo County

SCOPE OF THE BOOK

The intent of this book is to read a particular landscape: the alluvial fan of Putah Creek. It is not spectacular scenery—Yosemite Valley, or San Francisco Bay seen from the summit of Angel Island—but only an ordinary landscape, remarkably flat country devoted to farming, with some mountains in the distance. It is a landscape that would do little to pique the attention of a passing traveler. But it is a landscape that I know well.

I have collected my data not so much from archives as from field work—walking around for fifty years—east, west north, and south—looking at what's going on. I've worked in the countryside picking fruit, hoeing weeds, cutting firewood, planting orchards, driving a tractor, building barns and dismantling barns, and tending irrigation; much of this work requires only a moderate level of attention, and so I have been able to study my surroundings. For a while I ran an ad in the Winters newspaper offering to buy abandoned buildings for salvage, and in this way I came to know intimately several old barns, tank towers, and houses, as I carefully deconstructed them. There is not a house or barn in the district that I have not studied with a critical eye toward its architectural merits, and social history, and value as salvage.

As well as making my own observations, I have informally interviewed a number of old timers in the district, listening to their reminiscences of how things used to be and how the countryside used to function. Not all of their memories are in agreement, and in some cases I have had to make a guess based on plausibility as to what might be true.

In addition to a scarcity of archival references, there is another sense in which my approach is not strictly academic. The academician prides himself on his disinterest and dispassion. He is an observer and an outsider, objectively (he likes to think) recording a phenomenon. But I write as an insider and a member of the community, which entitles me to hold opinions, and to make judgments. And so I write in part as an activist, with my own notion of where things have gone wrong, and how they might be fixed, and where danger lurks and how it might be averted.

One other point: there is no simple name for the region I wish to discuss. Its boundaries are imprecise, and they fluctuate depending on my purpose. In a few instances I have wandered miles from the territory to get a needed photograph. It is awkward at best to keep saying, 'Putah Creek from Winters to Davis and the land for a few miles to either side,' or, 'the land within two hours walk of Stevenson Bridge.' So I am going to refer to it as 'the district.' This term is not technically valid in that Putah Creek divides Solano County to the south from Yolo County to the north, so that no formal jurisdiction encompasses the region. But as long as we agree on its use, 'district' will do.

Figure 3. Map of California, indicating the region of study.

Chapter Two:

Earth

THE SETTING

The central half of California is occupied by a huge, flat valley, 430 miles long and 70 miles wide at its widest. The Great Valley is not a valley in the conventional sense—a U-shaped or V-shaped channel dug into high ground by the erosive action of a river. The valley was at one time flat ocean bottom. It was lifted above sea level by tectonic activity, and became a broad coastal plain. Then, little by little, its four boundaries were set into place. The Sierra Nevada mountains arose to the east; the coast range, scraped from the surface of the subducting Pacific plate, formed to the west; the transverse range of the Tehachapi mountains blocked the southern end of the valley; and Mt Shasta, part of the volcanic Cascade range, plugged the northern end of the valley.

For much of its recent geologic history, the Great Valley was an inland sea. Even as recently as a century ago it was seasonally flooded in winter and spring. In wet years, an overland passenger from San Francisco to Sacramento had to trek far to the north, crossing the valley near the Sutter Buttes, and then travel southward along the foothills of the Sierra, finally dropping into Sacramento along the American River. The more direct route was impassable because of flooding.

The valley drains more than half of California's surface. Unlike a typical valley, with a river running along the center and an estuary at one end, the Great Valley has two principal rivers, one flowing north and one south, with a common estuary near the middle of the valley. This unique arrangement can be attributed to the unconventional geologic origin of the valley. From north to south the valley may be divided into thirds. The northern third is the Sacramento Valley, drained by the south-flowing Sacramento River; the middle third is the San Joaquin valley, drained by the north-flowing San Joaquin River; and the southern third is the Tulare Basin. The rivers feeding the Tulare basin do not join the San Joaquin, but instead supplied two large inland lakes—Tulare and Buena Vista, which were drained in the twentieth century (but which may be expected to reappear in a hundred-year flood). The watershed between the San Joaquin valley and the Tulare Basin is only a few dozen feet higher in altitude than the surrounding lands, so that the division is a subtle one.

If a geographer would divide the valley into its northern and southern parts, a farmer would find a more meaningful division to be the east side from the west side. On the east side the high Sierra Nevada mountains hold a permanent snow-pack, and abundant soft water flows from the east side throughout the year. The soils on the east side—overlapping alluvial fans of these rivers—are built from erosion of the Sierra Nevada's granite bedrocks, and tend to be acidic. On the west side, there is no permanent snow pack, and river flow is less dependable. In the Tulare basin and San Joaquin Valley, where the Sierras are higher, the coast range lower, and rainfall is scant, there are no year-round streams flowing from the west. The greater activity of the east-side rivers has pushed the San Joaquin river to the west of center, so that most of the valley is east side, with only a strip of west-side land. In the Sacramento valley, the coast range is higher, the Sierras lower, and rainfall is greater, so that the east-side rivers are balance by three year-round rivers flowing from the west side—Stony Creek, Cache Creek, and Putah Creek. The Sacramento River is more nearly centered in the valley, with the west side as wide as the east side. Rivers and alluvial fans on the west side derive from the mountains of the coast range—accretions of ancient ocean-bottom debris. The water is hard, and soils often are alkaline.

In addition to the North-South division and the east side-west side division, there is one other geographic division of the valley that merits comment: that is the division between the center of the valley and the periphery. The central region, extending approximately from Woodland in the north to Modesto in the south, is subject to marine influence in the form of nightly ocean breezes during the warmer seasons. The territory cooled by the Delta breeze may have 100 degrees of heat on a summer day, but drops comfortably into the 50's at night. Farther north or south, the temperature is still 90 at midnight. This division is relevant not only to the comfort of humans and animals, but to the growth of crops.

The subject of this book is a small region (approximately 45,000 acres) in the lower Sacramento valley, on the west side of the valley, well within the zone of marine influence. A small river, Putah Creek, known to the Spanish as Rio de los Putos, marks the center of the territory.

FLATNESS OF THE LAND

The landscape in this region is everywhere a variation on a theme: horizontal lines of vegetation, distant mountains, sky. The photographer peering into his viewfinder, or the landscape painter studying her empty canvas, must decide where the line of the horizon is to go. It belongs almost to the bottom of the frame, so that the picture is nearly all sky, with just a thin stack of lines at the lower edge.

The flatness of the land in the Great Valley is one of its most distinctive traits. The change in altitude in the central Putah Creek region is about five feet in a mile, with a gentle slope to the southeast. And this extraordinary flatness extends over a tremendous region, some eleven million acres of the Great Valley.

At a scale of miles, the slope is a steady five feet to the mile. But on a finer scale, of yards or rods, the land is not naturally quite so flat. In aboriginal times the land had slight local contours: dips and swales, slight hills, vernal pools. This subtle topography has been flattened out by human activity. The motivation for leveling a field is to improve irrigation. If a field is to be furrow irrigated, it must be very close to flat in order for the water to move evenly down the furrows. The ideal slope depends on the crop, the permeability of the soil, and the rate at which water is supplied to the head of the furrow. And so farmers level their fields. Earlier this was done with a land plane, an implement about sixty feet long, or even longer, with a blade at the center, that could be used to knock down humps and fill in hollows of the land. More recently, the land is leveled by setting a laser on a tower in the center of the field. A tractor pulls a scraper around the field which receives the laser signal, calculates its elevation, and raises or lowers its blade accordingly.

Most of the land in the district has been leveled at some time, but there are a few parcels that have not been, and they give us a notion as to the topography in aboriginal times. There is a 160 acre field at the corner of road 32 and road 97 that was not leveled until 1997. Before it was leveled it had subtle rises, and curving swales, and in late winter, vernal pools could be found.

Figure 4. Furrow irrigation of tomatoes requires level land. Solano County

Leveling it was a brutal undertaking that went on for months, with heavy equipment working through the night, and dust covering the land for several miles around. Now the field is in alfalfa, and in wintertime it floods the road at the low corner, for leveling it has destroyed its ability to contain the rain falling on it.

The original topography is also seen in many of the rural roads that run along section lines. The roads were established in the nineteenth century, before land-leveling was common, and they may have dips and rises that are a record of the slightly undulating landscape of that time. The agricultural fields to either side have been leveled.

ABSENCE OF STONES AND ROCKS

The 'clink' of a plow against a stone is a sound unheard in these parts. The soils of the district are silty loams and clay loams, formed from erosion of the coast range hills. Storm-fed streams in the hills might rage through the canyons gathering stones and rocks, but they quickly lose their velocity and drop their load when they reach the flat land of the valley; only the finest particles are carried by slow-moving floodwaters into the valley. And so no stones or rocks are to be found in the district, except upstream, near the base of the hills, or deep below the soil surface, where they were deposited by violent floods of long ago.

In the absence of stones, there are no stone walls to be found in the district, nor stone buildings. A few misguided individuals have trucked in boulders from great distance to decorate their homesteads; these stones always look to me to be out of place, lonely and bewildered, floating uneasily on a three-hundred foot thick layer of loam. And

Figure 5. Leveling a field with a sixty-foot land plane. Yolo County

usually they are not correctly set. An old Japanese gardener once told me that for a stone to look right in the landscape, two thirds of it has to be underground. Few of the boulder-collectors have the courage to bury their purchase so deeply.

THE CARTESIAN TRANSFORMATION

Among the aboriginal inhabitants of the district, individuals or families might hold fishing rights to a particular spot, or harvest rights to particular trees or grasslands, but ownership of land was not conceived of. The notion of holding title to a piece of land did not enter the district until the era of Spanish dominion. In 1842 a land grant of 17,754 acres was made from Spain to John Wolfskill and his brothers. The name of this grant was the 'Rancho Rio de los Putos,' and included most of the eastern half of the Putah Creek alluvial fan. The story is often told how Wolfskill established the perimeter of his grant by riding on horseback and keeping to the lands where the wild grasses reached the horse's withers. This accounts for several seemingly unmotivated jogs in county Road 32, which was part of the original perimeter of Rancho Rio de los Putos. Examination of a soil map supports the story, for the jogs neatly evade some regions of poor soils.

Wolfskill was a skilled and ambitious farmer; he was also a real estate developer, and much of his income derived from subdividing his land and selling off the pieces. The survey of the original grant, and of its subsequent subdivisions, was based on a grid of straight lines. In flat country, surveying land into square or rectangular pieces is a logical and uncomplicated undertaking. And yet, it has a profound influence on the development and appearance of the landscape.

Although the native land is flat, its innate variations do not occur in shapes of squares and rectangles. The soil maps have not a straight line on them; they depict a highly irregular mosaic of curved areas. There is a thirty acre field with which I am quite familiar, and running diagonally across it is a strip of varying width, on the average about fifty feet, where the soil is different. I can make out this strip by a day or two difference in germination of a crop, and by the color of the foliage, and the height of the plants, and the timing of maturity. Perhaps there is an old gravelly riverbed underlying the topsoil, so that it drains a little more quickly. The mosaic of soils is a three-dimensional one, extending to great depth. I was having a well bored, and the driller found 318 feet of loam before encountering a water-bearing gravel layer. At another well only a few hundred yards away he had struck gravel at twenty feet and encountered nothing but gravel to 200 feet, where he stopped. I asked the well driller what accounted for this variation. 'Worse than average luck,' he said.

After California became a state of the United States, the federal government surveyed the lands according to the township and range system championed by Thomas Jefferson. Section lines were laid out at one mile intervals, with their directions running north-south or east-west. Each section is one square mile, or 640 acres. The grid of Rancho Rio de los Putos, which predated the federal survey, was 26 degrees off the true cardinal directions, and so at the suture zone between the Rancho and the township survey one finds roads that do not meet at right angles, and trapezoidal and triangular parcels of land.

An odd oversight in the township and range survey is that no provision is made for roads. Usually, the owners of the land on each side of a section line grant easements of two rods (33 feet) in width, so that a net easement 66 feet wide with the section line running up the middle is available for roads. In general, it is to the farmer's advantage to have roads along his land, but not everyone agrees, and the easements sometimes are not granted, and the grid of section line roads is not complete.

The lack of congruence between soil maps and parcel maps is well known to farmers. They come to know their land well, and recognize that despite its flatness and seeming uniformity, the soils are variable. And so they adjust their practices accordingly. Some heavier ground might be planted to walnuts, and an adjacent area of lighter soils might be planted to almonds. The boundary of these two orchards reflects the soil map rather than the parcel map. The very large parcels on the map in Figure 6 are not farmed as single fields, but are planted in smaller plots according to the distribution of soils.

PARCEL SIZE AND THE TEXTURE OF LANDSCAPE

Before zoning laws were established, land was subdivided in an ad hoc manner. In general, the purchaser was interested in establishing a farm, and he would seek out a piece that was big enough to support a reasonable enterprise. But in more modern times, many urban people became interested in having a small plot of country land, not for livelihood, but for amenity. And to avoid a chaotic chopping up of the countryside into inconsistent parcels, zoning laws were put into effect. The underlying philosophy is that rural land should not be subdivided into parcels that are too small for the owner to earn a living by farming. In most of the Putah Creek alluvial fan, a size of forty acres is reckoned to be the minimum economic unit. On poor land, such as occurs in the foothills, the minimum size is increased to 160 acres.

What constitutes an economically sound parcel size varies with fluctuating markets and changes in technology. On good soils of the district, a competent farmer can earn a living from only forty acres growing fresh market fruits and vegetables. For some labor-intensive specialty crops (herbs, flowers, berries, nursery stock) five acres suffices. On the other hand, for a farmer who grows dryland grain and hay crops, even 300 acres is not enough to earn a fair living.

The parcel map of the district shows a number of small parcels that had been subdivided before zoning laws were in effect, together with a number of larger parcels that could in principle be further divided. The distribution of parcel sizes is critical in determining the texture of the landscape. Where there is a small parcel, there will be a house, and where there is a house, there will be trees. And so a cluster of small parcels results in a landscape that has the appearance of a woodland. The horizon is hidden; views are interrupted; one feels closed in. The maintenance of big fields of a few hundred acres or more is essential to preserve the generous spaciousness and open feeling of the countryside.

In other parts of the country where zoning laws are weak and are easily breached, the former agrarian landscape has been chopped up into a visual chaos of developments. Pinellas County, Florida, and Orange Country, California, are examples of the irretrievable destruction of a once-beautiful place by thoughtless subdivision of land. In the Putah Creek alluvial fan the agrarian landscape is relatively well preserved. Local governments have been commendably resistant to pressure from would-be developers who would like to subdivide the land (to their own considerable profit). To many of us, the rural landscape has an aesthetic and cultural value equal, in a subtle way, to the national parks, and we see it as being equally worthy of preservation.

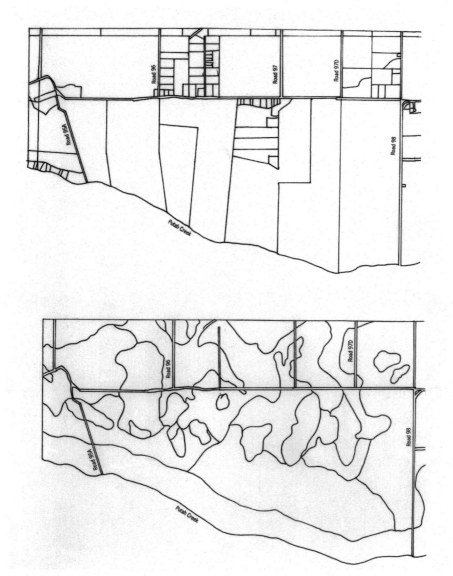

Figure 6. Parcel map (above) and soil map (below) of a small region in southern Yolo County. Only at the jog in road 95A do parcel lines and soil lines coincide.

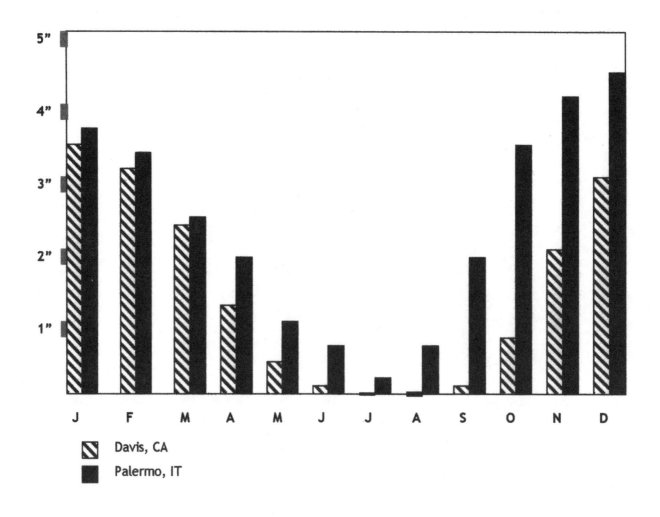

Figure 7. Average monthly rainfall in Davis, California and Palermo, Sicily.

Chapter Three:

Water

RAIN

Water enters the Putah Creek watershed as life-giving rain. Once a decade or so there may be a light dusting of snow, that persists for only a few hours. Equally rare is hail accompanying a late spring or early summer storm.

Rain is to be expected between November and April, with December, January, and February the wettest months. In June, July, and August, almost no rain falls. The pattern of dry summers and winter rains is referred to as a Mediterranean climate. Figure seven shows the average monthly distribution of rainfall at Davis, California (38° 32' N latitude) and at Palermo, Sicily (38° 06'N latitude). Although the curves are of similar shape, the seasonality in Palermo is not as extreme. In the six month period from May through October, Davis has an average of 1.53 inches of rain compared to Palermo with 8.2 inches. This is the basis for the remark that 'California is more Mediterranean than the Mediterranean itself.'

The pattern of winter rainfall, summer drought, is a critical determinant of the natural landscape. Plants make their growth in spring (February to May) and become dormant, or if they are annuals, die, in summer. Some trees, such as the California buckeye, are deciduous, losing their leaves as early as June as a means of avoiding the drought-stress of summer. I was once showing a visitor from Pennsylvania around the region in August, and he exclaimed, 'But everything's dead!' Because almost all land in the region is now irrigated, the droughtiness of summer is not as evident as it was in the aboriginal landscape.

To say, blandly, that no rain falls from May to October is one thing: to experience it is something

---

Water says: Wherever you put me, I'll be in my home. I am awfully smart. Lead me out of my springs, lead me from my rivers, but I came from the ocean and I shall go back into the ocean. You can dig a ditch and put me in it, but I go only so far and I am out of sight. I am awfully smart. When I am out of sight I am on my way home.

Wintun Indian woman, as told to Demetrocopolou, 1935.

And it never failed that during the dry years the people forgot about the rich years, and during the wet years they lost all memory of the dry years. It was always that way.

John Steinbeck, *East of Eden*, 1952

Figure 8. Summer plowing creates clouds of dust. Solano County

else. Late in spring hundreds of seasonal farm roads are established in the district, ringing each field, and as summer progresses the passage of trucks and tractors grinds the surface of these roads to a mulch of powdery dust. On breezy days, dust blows across the country, coating everything. On still days, dust hangs in the air for half an hour after a pickup has passed. The roofs of buildings lose their color and become a pale brown, the color of the earth. Dust dulls the leaves of trees, and coats the plums hanging heavily in the orchards. Day after day the sky is without clouds, so lacking in moisture that it seems the blueness has been baked out of it. Merciless sunlight bleaches the grasses until they are nearly white, bleaches the surfaces of buildings, the paint of cars, the retinas of animals' eyes. Where the land is not irrigated, the trees seem stunned by the dryness, their metabolisms contracted to a hard core of endurance.

With the first rainfall, in October, the landscape is as much transformed as New England is by autumn's first snowfall. Colors are brighter, almost garish compared to their restraint under a layer of dust. And where before the leaves of trees were a uniform dusty brownish green, there are now dozens of shades of green and gold. The air has been scrubbed, one feels like breathing deeply. The mountains seem closer, finely engraved with detail. It is as if one had just had cataract surgery, and was seeing for the first time a world focused and brightened. The grimness of summer gives way to feelings of relief and hope.

Rainfall usually is gentle. Eight hours of steady rain leading to a total accumulation of less than an inch is not uncommon. Rarely storms with heavy rains may visit the region, but even then the hourly rate of rainfall is less than the heavy summer rains of the tropics and subtropics. A once-in-a-century storm dumped 13 inches of rain on Winters in forty-eight hours in February, 1940, but rainfall at such a rate is highly unusual.

DRAINAGE

The Putah Creek watershed covers some 800 square miles, and about three quarters of it is mountainous. After the early rains have saturated the mountain soils, subsequent rainfall runs off in rivulets and streams that coalesce to form Putah Creek. Where it enters the valley, near Winters, Putah Creek is a decent-sized river. The Spanish thought enough of it to call it a 'Rio.' Whoever first disdainfully called it a 'creek' must have seen it in September, when its flow is reduced. In flood it is as mighty as the Missouri river, a wide expanse of fast-moving muddy water with uprooted trees floating swiftly down the channel.

In addition to its charge of water from the mountains, the creek also accepts, or once accepted, water from the flatlands, most of it delivered from meandering streamlets too minor to merit a name. Before the land was leveled for farming, there were many shallow seasonal pools where runoff from a heavy rainfall would collect until it slowly percolated into the water table. There is now a haphazard system of man-made drains along the edges of fields that can shunt runoff into the creek or into any of the various sloughs in the region. But seasonal pools, mostly unintended and inconvenient to humans, still collect rainfall on the flatlands in a wet year.

Putah Creek does not have a well-defined estuary. Formerly it simply spread out into the vast tule swamp that occupied the center of the Great Valley. In wet years the swamp was larger, in a period of drought it would contract. Now the creek peters out into a series of sinks, disappearing under ground.

In the 1950's Monticello Dam was built a few miles upstream of Winters. Its purposes were flood control and storage of water for irrigation. The dam averages out the flow of water in the creek between

Figure 9. Construction of an irrigation pipeline. Solano County.

Figure 10. *An irrigation canal brings Cache Creek water to within one hundred feet of Putah Creek. Yolo County*

wet season and dry season, and between wet years and dry years. Prior to the construction of the dam, flood waters from the creek were a powerful and regular force shaping the land, depositing and removing soil. In the flood of February, 1940, a whirlpool several hundred feet in diameter formed on the Phillips Ranch about seven miles downstream from Winters. When the waters receded, a large, saucer-shaped depression several feet deep in the center was found where the whirlpool had been. Undoubtedly this type of geomorphic process had been going on in the district for thousands of years, contributing to the complex three-dimensional distribution of soil types.

IRRIGATION

To a farmer, the Mediterranean climate has the advantages of a high summer light level because of the absence of clouds, and much reduced problems with plant disease because of the dry air and lack of rain. But the soil is dry in summer, and crops will not grow unless they are irrigated. And so much investment, public and private, and much labor and ingenuity have been expended in developing systems of irrigation. As an element of the landscape, irrigation is conspicuous by the many devices used for moving water around—canals, pipelines, weirs, sluices, ditches, furrows, sumps, pumps, standpipes, sprinklers, drip lines, siphons. Most of the summer work of farming in this district consists of tending irrigation.

There are two sources of irrigation water: the great underground lake of groundwater, and water entering the district through Putah Creek. Because the land slopes to the southeast, Putah Creek water moved in surface canals goes south and east into Solano county, but not northward into Yolo County. Canal water in Yolo County, even within sight of Putah Creek, comes from Cache Creek to the north. Not all farms are supplied with district water through a canal or pipeline, and even those that are cannot depend on that source in a drought year, and so many farms have wells. Wells are impressive engineered structures, some more than a thousand feet in length, but the interesting parts are all underground, and what the traveler sees is the pump, and the stream of water.

Figure 11. Sprinkler irrigation of onions. Yolo County

If you're walking the countryside in July and you come across a ditch full of water, it is an irrigation canal. And if you're walking in January and you find a flowing ditch, it's a drain. But in October, when everything is dry, it's not always easy to tell, unless you walk downstream for a ways. The canal is an artery; as one goes downstream it divides into smaller and smaller branches. A drain is a vein, and as one goes downstream it combines with other incoming drains to form a larger drain.

Figure 12. Roof-top wind vane. Yolo County

Chapter Four:

Air

I have heard it said that fish are unaware of the water in which they swim. I don't see how anyone who is not a fish could know this, but I suspect it is wrong. Like fish, we move in a fluid medium (air), and we are often aware of it. You turn a corner on your bicycle and you know quite well if it's a headwind or a tailwind you've picked up. You feel the slightest movement of air on your cheek, and the subtlest change in its temperature. Just a few molecules in the airstream as we inhale suffice to alert us to a distant fire, or to a Daphne bush blooming in the next block. As a visual landscape element, we notice the air by the action of the wind, and in clouds, and smoke and fog.

WIND

The district has two winds: the north wind and the south wind. The north wind is an evil wind. It scours the landscape, gathering strife and sowing discord. A four-day blow of north wind sets lovers to quarreling, drunkards to drinking, and the dog to sulking under the porch. There is a particular rhythm to the north wind. Often it starts in the small hours of the morning. You can hear it rattling the leaves in high treetops before it is felt at ground level. By dawn it is blowing hard, and keeps it up all day. And then, at dusk, the wind abates and there is a moment of peace. Then, it slowly starts up again and blows through the night. The north wind is gusty; it blows steadily at thirty or forty knots, but now and again kicks and punches at higher speeds. It is these malicious gusts that rip limbs from the trees, lodge wheat in the fields, tear shingles from the roof, and batter the fruit on the bough.

    Big blows of north wind occur most commonly in spring and fall, in the months flanking an equinox. A mid-summer north wind would be very unusual. And a mid-winter north wind harbors the arrival of a front of Alaskan air, but it is neither as strong nor as long-blowing as the fall and spring winds.

No evil is unalloyed, and I have learned to like the north wind, or at least not to dislike it so much. For once the internal combustion engine is not the dominant sound of the countryside, and the foot-traveler can feel himself to be in a primeval world, albeit an agitated one. The wind roars, mighty trees flail their limbs, and crows are blown sideways downwind like tatters of black paper. By the second day, if the dust has been settled by rain, the air becomes extraordinarily clear. Mountains eighty or a hundred miles away seem to be right before one, and fine details of the coast range are highly focused.

Winds from the south, (or more typically, the south-east) are of an entirely different character. They are ocean winds, with a soothing hint of moisture to them. In the summer, the south breeze, (the 'Delta breeze') comes up in the late afternoon, blows the day's heat away, and cools the valley down for the night. The Delta breeze makes valley life comfortable in the summer. The district of Putah Creek is finely situated to catch the Delta breeze; further south it blows hard and relentlessly. And thirty miles further north it is undependable, and frequently fails to arrive.

In the course of a summer day, heat expands the valley air, causing it to rise, and its pressure to drop. The ocean air, cooled by proximity to the water, is denser. And so a gradient of pressure between heavy ocean air and light valley air is the driving force of the Delta breeze. But although the ocean lies to the west of the district, movement of air from the west is blocked by the coastal mountains. Instead, the ocean air finds a sea-level route through San Francisco bay and up the channel of the Sacramento River before turning northward and westward, so that it comes to us from the south east. In years when the ocean is cooler than normal ('La Nina' currents), we have strong Delta breezes and a cool summer.

Rain also comes to us on a southeast wind. Even though the storm is coming from the north, from the gulf of Alaska, and its arrival is preceded by a north wind, when the storm reaches us bearing rain, the rain comes invariably from the southeast, following the same route as the Delta breeze.

I have rigged up a sort of recording anemometer so that on the morning following a windy night I can check to see how hard the wind has blown. There is a place where sometimes at the end of the day we sit and talk and have a drink, and we set the empty bottles atop a fence. A wind of twenty knots will blow a beer bottle off; thirty-five knots takes a Riesling bottle; forty knots a cabernet bottle; and a gust of sixty knots is needed to blow a champagne bottle off the fence.

FOG

Tule fogs of the winter months are a characteristic feature of the Great Valley. If you hike up into the hills, gaining a thousand or fifteen hundred feet of altitude, you emerge into bright sunshine and blue skies. Looking back into the valley is like looking into a bowl of marshmallows or beaten egg whites—a dense whiteness. In the valley, on the ground, the light is subdued, colors are muted, everything seems shades of gray, as if one moved in a black-and-white photograph. Walking along one is surprised by the closeness of objects that suddenly loom. It is a landscape congenial to a pessimist.

Like falling snow, fog muffles sound, and on foggy days the land is quiet. Standing on a ladder in an orchard, pruning apricot trees, I hear only the calls of crows, and the sound of my loppers slicing off branches. The quietness of the scene, and the absence of any man-made thing more sophisticated than a ladder, afford me the fantasy that I have been transported back into the thirteenth century. When as a child I first heard the term 'the dark ages,' I at once acquired an ineradicable notion that for several hundred years the sun did not shine brightly. And so on this subdued and dark day I look to my feet half expecting to find some crude, handmade sandals, and to hear distant church bells, and to see my neighbor coming down the path in an oxcart.

Even a slight bit of wind will dispel fog. The turbulence in the air tumbles the tiny droplets of water together; they coalesce, and become heavy, and drop to the ground. An hour of a rising breeze is enough to disperse a dense fog. But there are times when the weather system is static; there is no breeze, and the fog persists for days, rising to a hundred feet or so in the late afternoon, and then quickly descending back to earth after sundown. When fog persists for days, the citizens become introspective and morbid. They long for light, for colors. The fog engulfs them like a clinical depression, with the blueness of the sky just beyond, remembered but unreachable.

The drivers of cars don't know how to behave in fog. Some drive sixty, unconcerned that they cannot see where they are going. Others poke along at ten miles per hour. Wrecks are common.

Fog that has made itself at home for a period of days may rise in the afternoon, permitting visibility of a mile or so, and then it settles like a dropped blanket again in the evening. But fog newly forming after a period of clear weather arrives differently. If it is a moonlit night, the foot-traveler in the country a few hours after sunset will notice the first fog forming as threads, strings, tubes, sheets. Ribbons of fog move slowly across a field, a few feet off the ground, or snake eerily through an orchard. This does not happen everywhere at once. Certain places are prone to early fogs. There is a topography to the air more complex than the topography of the utterly flat land. Parcels of cold air slide and tumble from the mountains of the coast range, and enter the valley with a trajectory determined by the slant and cut of the hills and rifts, and by the placement of buildings and trees. Currents and eddies and backwashes follow defined paths, and one comes to learn certain places where first the fog forms, and characteristic ways in which it moves. This is information useful to a farmer or a gardener, for it shows him the cold spots on his place, and by subtraction he then knows the warm spots as well.

Figure 13. Tule fog—road to nowhere. Solano County

I remember in elementary school waiting with my sister for the school bus on foggy mornings. We stood under dripping walnut trees on country road 32, straining eyes and ears eastward. We saw the blinking yellow light before we heard the muffled puttering of the engine. The bus would glide to a stop, the door would swing open, and we would climb aboard. The driver would grind the gears and the bus would move into the swirling fog, while we peered out the windows, feeling snug in our yellow submarine.

CLOUDS

In the matter of clouds, the district is deprived. Winter clouds often are too close; they descend upon us and engulf us, as fog, and we cannot see them as clouds because we are too near. In the summer months, we may go for ten weeks at a stretch without a cloud; just merciless blue sky, day after day. And then, as fall approaches, you look up one day and there they are, gliding silently across the sky like sailing ships arriving unexpectedly at a neglected harbor.

Some study clouds with an analytical eye, seeking to foretell the weather. The citrus grower whose tangerine crop is still half unpicked in January looks happily on clouds, for when there are clouds there will not be a frost. But even to one who cares little about the weather, there is something irresistible about clouds. Never will you see anything so large in motion—even the biggest ocean liner is puny by comparison. And the motion of the clouds is mirrored by the march of shadows across the land.

In other regions, clouds regularly enact a drama that is metaphorical for much of human life. There is an ominous gathering of clouds, confrontation and shoving amongst them, darkening, then an outburst of lightning, violent thunder, a catharsis of rain, and a renewed peace. This too, we miss. In the district of Putah Creek there is not a thunder storm once in twenty years. And so we are deprived of a celestial dramatization of our daily lives. Even the most mundane task—hoeing weeds, shaking out a rug—becomes theatrical when the backdrop is gliding piles of clouds, and slanting shafts of sunlight.

Figure 14. Towers for high-voltage electrical wires. Solano County

Chapter Five:

Fire

In the primeval landscape, fires resulted from lightning strikes. Lightning is infrequent in the district, and fires originating locally must have been uncommon. However, since there are hardly any natural barriers to the spread of fire in the Great Valley, a strike anywhere in the valley or surrounding foothills might set off a blaze that would burn tremendous areas. Within the confines of the Putah Creek alluvial fan, fires most likely arrived from the north, pushed along by a north wind, consuming the accumulated thatch of prairie grasses and tules. Occasional fires, together with grazing animals (antelope, deer, and elk) and periodic flooding, maintained the savannah and prairie vegetation of the district.

After humans settled, fires were set deliberately to aid in hunting. Strategically placed hunters would catch the grasshoppers and small animals that were fleeing the advancing flames. Fires also were set to stimulate a particularly lush crop of grass the following spring, which would attract antelope and deer. In addition, small plots of ground were burned off in preparation for planting tobacco. Undoubtedly some of these fires burned out of control and consumed bigger tracts than had been intended.

In the twentieth century, setting fires has been a regular farming practice, especially for burning off corn stalks and rice stubble, and for disposing of orchard prunings. Concern for preventing air pollution is forcing abandonment of these practices; corn is now mowed with a flail mower and then plowed under, rice straw is baled and the stubble buried, and orchard prunings often are chipped and left to decay on the orchard floor. However, the transition is not complete, and on days when burning is permitted you can see tall columns of white smoke across the countryside, and catch a whiff of the pleasant smell of burning straw.

THE ELECTRICAL GRID AS A LANDSCAPE ELEMENT

Fire is a transformation of chemical energy (in the unburned fuel) into radiant energy (light and heat). We can take a broader interpretation of the word 'fire' to include other transformations of energy. The most important fire to us is the sun, where atomic energy is transformed to radiant energy (light and heat) that reaches the earth. A small bit of the light is captured by plants in photosynthesis, the fueling step for all plants and animals. The sun's energy also powers the weather systems, evaporating water from the oceans and driving the winds. Water flowing down a mountain has kinetic energy, some of which may be transferred to a turbine at a power plant to make electrical energy, which is transmitted through wires to distant users.

The distribution of electricity is the single most conspicuous feature of the man-made environment in the district. There is no square mile, and perhaps not even any quarter section, which is not surrounded and traversed by poles and wires. The photographer who wishes to record a rural scene unpunctuated by utility poles is out of luck; the only option is to remove them digitally before the image is printed. In addition to the local electrical grid, there are several trunk lines transmitting electricity across the region at high voltages, the power flowing from north to south. These long lines of outsized steel towers seem like something imagined in the science fiction of the 1950's.

Most people have never seen a landscape that did not have utility poles, with their connecting wires hanging in gentle parabolas, and so take no notice of them. And yet, if the electrical grid were to be removed, I think that most would find

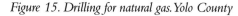

Figure 15. Drilling for natural gas. Yolo County

the landscape improved, even if they couldn't say why. In the 1970's I was working in the province of Junin, in Peru, and there were lovely valleys in the mountains that had small towns in them with no electricity or telephones, and no advertising or signs. That landscape was irresistible. It was as if the eye and the mind were unburdened of an annoyance, and life could be carried out in a way both simple and true.

OIL & GAS

An inattentive traveler would hardly notice the petroleum industry of the district. There is no oil here, no derricks, none of those curious bobbing pumps that one sees in other parts of the country. But the district does have natural gas, and from time to time a gas drill rig will be set up for a few weeks, its high tower topped with a cluster of blinking lights. And then one day the rig is disassembled and trucked away, the ground is graded flat, and there is nothing much left to see. If the well was a success, an underground pipeline will be brought out to it within a year or so, and at the well head a tank will be placed and a labyrinthine knot of pipes, valves, and meters assembled. A chain link fence is put around the plot, with a heavy padlock on the gate. Once in a great while someone will check the meter, to monitor flow and calculate royalties. The farmer adjusts his plowing pattern to swerve around the installation. There are dozens of these little well-head stations in the rural district—the new ones shiny, the old ones rusting.

Figure 16. Natural gas wellhead, with wild walnut trees, in winter. Yolo County

Figure 17. Windbreak of Lombardy poplars protecting orchards of Asian pears. Yolo County

Chapter Six:

Vegetation

> I like trees because they seem more resigned to the way they have to live than other things do.
> Willa Cather,
> *O Pioneers!*, 1913

> All Nature is so full, that that district produces the greatest variety which is most examined.
> Gilbert White,
> *Natural History of Selbourne,* 1768

VEGETATION IN 1800

Although by 1800 humans had been living in the Putah Creek alluvial fan for some thousands of years, their influence on the vegetation probably was slight. Humans were few, their technology was simple, and agriculture was minimal. And so the vegetation at that time differed little from the pre-aboriginal vegetation.

Two long ribbons of land adjacent to Putah Creek supported a dense riparian forest. Closest to the creek were willows, and not far off their cousins, cottonwoods. Farther from the channel were black walnuts, and also box elders (a type of maple). On higher ground the dominant tree was the valley oak. On the high ground, but near the creek, the vegetation was an oak woodland—a fairly open forest of nearly pure stands of valley oak, with a few cottonwoods and walnuts mixed in, and a low understory of perennial grasses. A shrubby undergrowth, typical of eastern forests, was absent, and travel through the oak woodland by humans on foot was unimpeded.

Moving away from the creek, both north and south, the valley oaks were further and further apart, the intervening space being occupied by a perennial prairie comprised mostly of grasses. This type of vegetation is an oak savannah, arbitrarily distinguished from an oak woodland by a cover of trees which occupies less than thirty percent of the land. With increasing distance from the creek the savannah gave way to open prairie, with a dominant bunchgrass, *Stipa pulchra,* and a number of other grasses, also with a bunching habit. As in other regions, persistence of the prairie depended on grazing by large mammals (antelope, elk, and deer) and also rodents, and on periodic fires.

Figure 18. Prodigious cottonwood tree left standing in a prune orchard. Solano County

In the eastern half of the alluvial fan the prairie graded into tule marsh, the dominant vegetation of the central part the Great Valley. The tule marshes were inundated for about half of the year, which favored the growth of tules over the prairie grasses.

VEGETATION IN 2000

In the year 2000 the riparian forest remains, although in places it is badly degraded both by cutting of the trees and by invasion of exotics. Tamarisk, ailanthus, eucalyptus, and alien willows have made inroads and are pushing out the natives. On higher ground, the oak woodland, oak savannah, and prairies have almost entirely vanished. That land now is all in agriculture. There are still scattered native trees to be found—walnuts, cottonwoods, and mighty oaks, but their numbers are ever diminishing.

If we reckon orchards to be woodland, then the acreage of woodland has probably increased since 1800. In aboriginal times, the limiting factor on spread of forest was availability of water. With irrigation, trees can prosper where formerly they would have failed. The towns, too, have a forest-like vegetation, with nearly complete tree cover in the older parts of town. Pastureland is similar to the original prairies, although its species composition is now very different. There are several other perennial herbaceous crops—notably alfalfa, but also asparagus, that are have a slight similarity to the prairies. But most of the non-orchard land is now in annual crops. In the aboriginal vegetation, annuals played a very minor role, but modern field crops and row crops are all annuals. The weeds, too, are mostly annuals, and non-cultivated parts of the countryside are heavily infested with annual weeds of Eurasian origin.

Much of the former tule swamp is now farmed. This has been achieved partly by drainage projects but primarily by damming the rivers that flow into the valley, so that winter flooding is much reduced from what it had been. Nonetheless, there are patches of tules persisting in swampy spots in the district.

From a purely visual point of view, the greatest change in the landscape is that the land is now divided into squares and rectangles, and in the arrangement of plants straight lines are the dominant feature. Although the primeval landscape had a logic and order to it, it was not an order in which straight lines played any part.

A FEW NOTABLE PLANTS

Of the genus *Populus*—the poplars, cottonwoods, and aspens—two species are prominent in the district. The native cottonwood, *Populus fremontii,* is common along the creek, and here and there on higher ground. The most charming feature of this tree is its foliage. The leaves are heart-shaped, deep green in summer and a clear yellow in autumn, and their stalks are flattened so that they flutter in the slightest breeze, and rustle very pleasingly in a higher wind. The lumber is weak and of little value for construction or even firewood, but it is much esteemed by beavers, of whom it is the favorite food. In parts of the creek where beavers are plentiful, the cottonwoods are constantly under attack. There is a very fine old cottonwood, the trunk some eight feet in diameter, on high ground in Solano County not far from Stevenson Bridge.

The other common poplar is the Lombardy poplar (*Populus nigra var. italica*), an immigrant from Italy. Long rows of it have been planted as windbreaks to protect tender crops (particularly Asian pears and kiwis) from cold north winds. Only the male of this tree is known, and is propagated by cuttings, which root readily. The Lombardy poplar is a short lived tree which after a couple of decades begins to die out and fall apart.

The California black walnut, *Juglans hindsii*, is most notable in the district for a magnificent avenue of hundred-and-thirty-year-old trees extending for more than a mile along Russell Boulevard in Yolo County. Despite a history of bad pruning they are handsome trees, and form a broad

Figure 19. Avenue of olive trees. Solano County

canopy over the roadway. The nuts are eagerly collected and stashed by birds and rodents, and have been spread around the countryside, so that young walnut trees may be expected to pop up in any hedgerow or fencerow. The shell of the nut is tough as iron, and all winter long crows tote them aloft and drop them from a height onto rural roads in hopes of cracking them. The black walnuts are particularly susceptible to infestation by mistletoe. This is most obvious in winter, when the walnut has shed its own leaves, and the clumps of green mistletoe are readily seen. The native black walnut is the preferred rootstock for the English walnuts that are grown commercially. So we the curious situation of thousands of acres of living black walnut roots, but not a leaf to be seen. The black walnut has dark, furrowed bark whereas the English walnut has smooth light gray bark; therefore, the position of the graft in the orchard trees is quite evident.

The olive, native to the Mediterranean, was brought to the district during the period of Spanish dominion. Its slender leaves are gray-green above and silver below, and when tossed by the wind the tree has a silvery sparkle to it. The olive is a long-lived tree—an unverified age of a thousand years often attributed to trees in their native region—and many of the original plantings in this area still thrive. It is only recently that olive orchards have been planted here; the tree was almost always used as a roadside tree, to line avenues and mark boundaries. The most appealing roads in the region are those bordered by olive trees that meet overhead in a gothic arch. Although the charm of these avenues is much admired, no one seems inclined to imitate it. I know of only one avenue of olives planted in the last eighty years. I planted it myself.

Modern landscape architects seem to have an aversion to formal avenues of trees. Instead, they plant a clump of sycamores, then half a dozen irregularly spaced flowering pears, then a few hackberries, and an odd grouping of pistache trees, and then back to the sycamores. The advantage of this is that if a tree dies, it is not much noticed, whereas in a formal avenue if one tree dies the discontinuity is obvious and troublesome. The lack of courage in planting avenues of a single species goes along with another modern weakness: a predilection for needlessly curved streets.

Eucalyptus, native to Australia, is now the dominant genus of trees in the Great Valley of California. It is possible to drive the full length of the valley, more than 400 miles, without ever being out of sight of a eucalyptus. The trees were first grown in San Francisco in 1856, and by 1860 the Nolan Nursery in Oakland was growing a dozen species in great numbers. Eucalyptus, noted for its extremely fast growth (ten feet or more per year in some cases) was thought to have great potential for production of railroad cross ties and bridge timbers. Seed was imported from Australia seemingly indiscriminately; more than eighty species were being grown by the 1880's, and planted willy-nilly around the state. Unfortunately, many of the species most widely planted were not the best for timber.

In the Putah Creek alluvial fan there are a number of eucalypts, most notable for their great height. They are the tallest trees in the district, some more than 140 feet tall. They are favored by hawks for building nests with a wide view. Most are hybrids involving *Eucalyptus viminalis, E. camaldulensis*, and perhaps a few others. They seed readily, and are an invasive pest in the riparian forest along the creek. Some are cut for firewood, which has a high heat value, and some are exported through the port of West Sacramento, where they are chipped as bulk raw material for the manufacture of oriented strand board, a common building material. A few exceptional trees are being sawed into lumber. It takes great skill to saw and season eucalyptus, and there is considerable waste, but the successful results are of great merit. I have a few hundred feet of eucalyptus boards seasoning in a shed.

The eucalypts have very deep roots. A pump repair man was complaining to me about difficulty he had pulling a pump that had become entangled in eucalyptus roots at a depth of seventy feet. With roots that deep, the trees are pumping considerable groundwater into the atmosphere. Indeed, they are planted specifically as pumps in parts of the San Joaquin valley where the water table is too high.

Although several dozen species

Figure 20. Palms, pines, and cypresses at an old homestead. Solano County

of palms are hardy in the district, only two are widely planted: *Washingtonia*, and the Canary Island Date. These were introduced early, and were much favored by settlers for dooryard plantings or short avenues leading to a house. Often, the only remaining sign of a vanished farmstead is a pair of date palms at the edge of a field. In the same breath as palms one might mention some of the conifers, particularly the deodar cedar and the Italian cypress. The relationship is not a botanical one but an architectural one; all of these are predictably symmetrical, and the regularity of their shape seems to have recommended them to gardeners of a certain frame of mind.

There is a native grape, *Vitis californica,* that grows in the riparian forest along the creek. It has handsome, nearly round leaves, silver below, with a dentate edge. The grapes are small, and almost all seed and skin, and not very sweet, but the birds are keen on them anyway. The cultivated grape vines one usually sees are so ferociously disciplined by hard pruning, that it is a pleasure to see an unrestrained wild grape scampering sixty feet up a tree and then hanging in the breeze.

The tule (*Scirpus acutus*), once common in the district, has nearly disappeared although there are still a few stands of it, often growing mixed with cat tails. It was used by the native peoples for thatching their dwellings, making baskets, and various other uses. The first white settler in the district, John Wolfskill, built a house of tules in 1842.

The valley oak, *Quercus lobata*, is the undisputed

Figure 21. Wayside valley oak tree, about 125 years old. Its further growth will be more horizontal than vertical so that over the next hundred years it will become wider than tall. Solano County

queen of trees in the district. It is not the tallest, seldom exceeding seventy feet, but it may have well more than a hundred feet of spread, and its branches grow in wide, crooked arches, with the farthest tips often hanging and nearly reaching the ground, so that one can step into the interior of the tree as if into the interior of a large green room. (In such a room one feels druidic stirrings, and an impulse to doff one's cap out of respect.) In the 1800's the valley oak was the commonest tree of the region, and even in the 1950's there were still many tremendous oaks scattered through the farmland. When livestock culture was more common, much of the farm land was in pasture, and leaving a few noble oaks as shade trees for livestock was reckoned a good practice. (Before the invention of the chainsaw these big trees were not so easily got rid of, either, so there was that advantage to just leaving them.)

The acorns of the valley oak were the principal food of the aboriginal peoples. They were gathered in early autumn and stored for year-round use. They are still a principal food of much of the wildlife—particularly birds and rodents. They sprout readily, and oak seedlings appear in hedgerows and other unplowed ground where the blue jays and squirrels have stashed the acorns and forgotten them.

An agricultural well was being bored near my place, and being interested in such things I was standing around watching the work. The men had brought a backhoe and dug a large pit to contain the drill mud. At a depth of about eight feet they encountered a mass of tree roots. The roots were about finger thickness, and running parallel to the surface of the ground and to each other. I got a piece of root and inspected the cut end—it had the distinctive anatomy of an oak. The nearest oak was a tremendous valley oak about a hundred and twenty feet away. The pit with the roots was a good fifty feet past the outermost aerial part of the oak tree. If this is typical, then a valley oak in a pasture has a root system several times larger than the area of its shadow at noon, and in an oak savanna all the ground is permeated with oak roots.

I once lived for a while in a small town in another state. One of the town characters was a woman who hugged trees. She was a young woman, perhaps thirty, and she wore unusual garments of her own invention consisting of lengths of cloth that she wrapped loosely around herself. I would be driving to the lumber yard to pick up a load of boards and spot her at the side of the road, embracing a laurel oak, her bare arms around its trunk, her cheek against its rough bark, a dreamy look on her face. An hour later, driving the opposite way, I'd look and she'd still be there, in the same position. She didn't hug lamp posts or telephone poles, or even palm trees; as near as I could tell she specialized in oaks. Perhaps she was simple, or perhaps her mind had been damaged by drugs. Among the townspeople, many rude jokes were made at her expense, but I did not share in them. I suspected that in her gentle and patient way she might be teaching us something fundamental, and we were too obtuse to understand the lesson.

Figure 22. Grain elevators storing feed corn. Solano County

Chapter Seven:

Agriculture

> **Until we understand what the land is, we are at odds with everything we touch.**
> Wendell Berry,
> *A Native Hill*, 1969

SUITABILITY OF THE LAND FOR FARMING

If one accepts the propositions (and many would not) that humans are a part of nature, and that farming is a natural activity of humans, then it follows that for some parts of the land agriculture is its natural state. Farming is not a perversion of nature, but a natural development in our planet's evolution.

The central Putah Creek district is especially favored for farming. The soils are fertile, stone-free, and deep. Rainfall in the watershed is sufficient that irrigated farming can be carried out without depleting geologic groundwater. This is because about three quarters of the watershed is mountainous and is not farmed, and runoff from that serves to irrigate the remaining arable quarter. The climate is cold enough to provide adequate chilling for stone fruits, yet warm enough that citrus can be profitably grown. Dryness of the air in the summer season makes the region inhospitable to plant diseases, which are much less prevalent than in more humid zones. Absence of clouds through much of the year guarantees high light intensity that supports rapid plant growth. The land is so flat that furrow irrigation is feasible. Rainfall is gentle; eight hours of rain totaling less than an inch is a typical rate. Flat land together with gentle rainfall mean that the risk of soil erosion is essentially zero; indeed, historically this is a zone of soil deposition. Farming practices that would be ecological felonies in other regions, such as leaving the earth plowed bare through the rainy season, may here be practiced seemingly without penalty. Finally, the native ecosystem was sufficiently simple, and of such wide extent, that it could have been reasonably preserved, with perhaps the exception of elk and antelope, by setting aside only a few percent of the district as a reserve. That this did not happen is unfortunate, but at least in principle conversion of a majority of the land to agriculture needn't have meant the extirpation of the native biota.

FOUR PERIODS OF FARMING

The aboriginal economy was one of hunting and gathering. Acorns from the valley oak (*Quercus lobata*) were the mainstay of the diet, supplemented by walnuts, wild grains, berries, and game: elk, antelope, jackrabbit, skunk, opossum, squirrel, mouse, quail, grasshopper, crayfish, and many kinds of fish from the creek. Agriculture in the narrow sense was restricted to tobacco, which was sown and cultivated on small plots.

The second wave of agriculture, extending from the era of Spanish dominion into the first decades of statehood, was one of grazing. Large herds of cattle, horses, and sheep were tended throughout the Great Valley, relying on the native prairie grasses as their principle forage.

The third wave of farming in the district, occupying the last quarter of the nineteenth century, was the rise of dryland grain farming. Vast tracts were planted to grain. The four-year crop rotation was wheat, wheat, wheat, wheat. Development of combines for harvesting, and establishment of railroads in the region, were the technological underpinnings of grain farming. Great Valley wheat was exported throughout the world.

The modern era of farming coincided with the introduction of irrigation pumps driven by fossil-fuel powered engines. This permitted irrigation of land, and establishment of orchards, vineyards, row crops, and irrigated forage. Abandonment of draft animals in favor of tractors allowed much land formerly in pasture and hay to be planted to cash crops.

The simple four-part history just given indicates the general trend in farming, but the specific details are much less orderly. For example, dry land orchards were established around Winters even during the Spanish era. And by 1860 a steam engine at Davis, and another at Winters, were pumping irrigation water from Putah Creek at a rate of about 600 gallons per minute at each site. All four agricultural systems survive today. Hunting and gathering is still common in the case of the native black walnut (*Juglans hindsii*). In the 1950's my friends and I gathered these nuts from native wild trees. Donnell's feed and grain store in Davis paid us a dollar per hundred pounds, and I made twenty or thirty dollars each season. Like many things that used to be considered children's work—mowing lawns, delivering newspapers, collecting bottles—gathering walnuts has now become a job for desperate adults. I see them, frowning and muttering as they work. Perhaps they are calculating how much the rent is overdue, and how many more sacks they must fill before it is too dark to see.

Grazing of cattle and sheep on unirrigated pasture continues on several parcels in the district, most notably the T.S. Glide ranch. Much of the grazing is restricted to local inclusions of poor soil in the Corning series (eroded gravelly loams). The quality of pasture is much degraded by overgrazing and invasion of yellow star thistle. In addition, livestock (sheep in particular) are sometimes grazed on residues of row crops after harvest.

Dry land grain farming is also still common in the district, with wheat, barley, and safflower being important crops. These usually are in a rotation with irrigated row crops, such as tomatoes, corn, beans, and squash.

FARMING FOR DOLLARS

The style of farming in the district differs greatly from the traditional farming style of the eastern states. An eastern farm was nearly a self-sufficient entity. Most of the farm labor was directed to satisfying the internal needs of the farm—food, buildings, clothing, utensils, and various amenities. Sale of products off the farm for cash was a minor part of the enterprise, and typically products of high value were sold—milk, eggs, meat, hides, and perhaps grains and fruit, often in the form of fermented beverages. But in the Putah Creek region, farming was strictly a cash enterprise, right from the outset. All the farm product (livestock, grain, fruit) was for sale, usually in distant markets, and the internal needs of the farm were met by purchasing whatever was needed. This had a profound effect on the agrarian landscape. The diversified small farm of east, with its correspondingly diverse landscape, is replaced instead by large tracts of monoculture.

There is a social dimension to this farm structure as well. The land is worked not by farmers but by workers, who have no ownership and no tenure. The farmer is a manager. And so there is a long history of a division between management and labor that foreshadows the industrial model of farming. This falls somewhere in between the masters-and-slaves plantation economy of the antebellum south, and the independent yeoman farmers of the northeastern quadrant of the country.

Figure 23. Mexican workers planting grape vines for nursery stock. Solano County

CROPS

The western half of the district is dominated by orchards. In the first two thirds of the twentieth century, stone fruits were the principal tree crops. Apricots, cherries, plums, peaches and nectarines were grown and the fruit was shipped to Eastern markets where fruit from Winters enjoyed a niche as the earliest California fruit. But with the rise of stone fruit culture in the San Joaquin valley, Winters lost the advantage of earliness, and gradually the apricot and peach orchards have been pulled out. Dominant now are walnuts, almonds, and prunes. These crops can be harvested mechanically, and so the problems of managing a large, itinerant labor force are obviated. In the 1990's, walnuts have been a solid money-maker, and thousands of acres in the district have been planted to walnuts. Minor orchard crops—pecans, pistachios, pears, figs, persimmons, and Christmas trees—are holding about steady, while acreage of citrus, apples, and olives is increasing.

Of the vineyard crops, kiwi fruit, which was once a high value crop in the district, is nearly extinct, a victim of over planting that led to prices that were below the cost of production. Grapes, on the other hand, have been increasing in acreage. Wine grapes (Barbera, Shiraz, and some Rhone varietals) are being planted here and there in the district. But even more acreage is given to growing grape vine root stocks as a nursery crop. The vines are sold as one or two-year-old rootings for grafting, or the grafted plants are grown out for a year before being dug for replanting elsewhere in the west.

The major row crop of the district has been tomatoes for processing; like walnuts, tomatoes have been steady money makers until the beginning of the twenty-first century, when closure of canneries and bankruptcy of the tomato growers' cooperative have rendered tomatoes unprofitable for many growers. Tomatoes are grown in rotation with wheat, either a two year rotation (wheat, tomatoes, wheat, tomatoes) or a five crop/four year rotation with corn, safflower, beans, and wheat. In the northern part of the district, where heavy, water-holding clay soils are found, rice is grown; this is the south-western border of the great rice district of the central Sacramento valley. Minor row crops include peppers, cabbage, broccoli, beans, asparagus, artichokes, green onions, storage onions, bok choi, fennel, collards, mustard, strawberries, and sweet corn. Sugar beets, once the equal of tomatoes in the district, have nearly disappeared due to the ravages of dis-

Figure 24. Pumpkins grown for seed. Yolo County

ease, low prices, and closure of refineries. Oil-seed crops are widely grown, including safflower, canola, and sunflowers.

Forage crops include irrigated pasture, oat hay, alfalfa, corn, milo, and sudan grass hay. Sudan is sometimes grown as a rotation with rice, as it can tolerate heavy soils. It can be cut four or five times a season—almost as much as alfalfa. Forage crops and pasture occupy about half of the land not planted to orchards.

There is considerable farming in the district devoted to production of agronomic seeds, that is, seeds that will be sold to other farmers for planting. Much of the sunflower production in the district is for seed; absence of wild sunflowers which could contaminate the crop by cross pollination is a favorable factor. Also grown for seed are sudan grass, asparagus, beets, carrots, onions, beans, tomatoes, peppers, rutabagas, canola, broccoli, and the whole melon tribe—squash, melons, pumpkins, and cucumbers. Crops grown for seed are held to high standards of cleanliness in the field; there is essentially zero tolerance of weeds, and the seed crops must be grown in spatial and temporal isolation from related crops by which they might be accidentally pollinated.

Finally, there are a number of small truck farms scattered through the district producing a great variety of vegetables, fruits, berries, herbs, and flowers for local markets.

Figure 25. Cultivating tomatoes. Solano County

LIVESTOCK

Grazing animals, whether wild or domesticated, have a characteristic way of moving about. The herd grazes a region and moves on, grazes and moves on. The farmer who would keep a dozen cows on a forty acre plot mimics this. He fences and cross-fences so that the plot is divided in quarters, and then moves the animals every few weeks to a new quarter, allowing the quarter just vacated an opportunity to recover. This works even on a small scale. A typical scene in country that has been divided into ranchettes is a one acre field of dust (or mud) with a bored lone horse standing in it. An acre is not enough ground for a horse. But if that acre were quartered, and the horse moved every three weeks, in its nine weeks of recovery time a quarter could be put back into presentable pasture, at least in the warm seasons, despite overstocking. There is very little livestock kept in the district, but what there is generally is overstocked; that is, too many animals are kept for the amount of grazing land.

Horses are most numerous, with about 250 head in the district; none of these is a working horse—they are kept for recreation. Fewer than a hundred cattle are to be found, varying with the season (not including about 140 head of cattle at the University of California). There is no dairy industry nearby, although dairy is the number one segment of California agriculture in revenues. A few small flocks of sheep are grazed, often with a llama or donkey added to the flock to deter coyotes; total numbers of sheep in the district are less than 200. There is a major sheep-raising area to the south in Solano county, of which these few flocks are the northern outliers. A few dozen goats lodge in the district—one herd, and a number of isolated individuals raised as 4H projects. Many rural residents keep a few hens and a rooster, but there is no commercial poultry raising. The population of pigs is zero. Bee-keeping is prominent, as many hives are required to pollinate the orchards (except walnuts, which are wind pollinated) and the crops grown for agronomic seeds

Figure 26. Cattle grazing—an unusual sight in the district. Yolo County

(sunflowers, melons, etc).

A century ago horses were far more common, serving as transportation and as draft animals (though mules were preferred for plowing). In order to maintain the horses and mules, about a third of the farm was given over to oat hay and pasture. The associated fences, gates, corrals, barns, and sheds were a characteristic part of the landscape. With the rise of the pickup truck and the tractor, the horses and mules lost their place in the rural economy. Acreage of pasture diminished, and many fences, corrals, and outbuildings were pulled down.

The absence of animals on farms in the district is contrary to the fundamental notion of a farm in most of the world, and signals an imbalance in farm ecology. It is particularly strange given that about half of the open (non-orchard) land is devoted to animal feed crops—alfalfa, sudan, and oat hay; milo; and corn. Except what is used by the horses in the district, all of this is destined for export to other parts of California and Nevada or to Japan.

Figure 27. Thirty-inch beds worked up in July. They will not be planted (with peppers) until the following April. Solano County

THE ANOMALY OF BARE GROUND

The soils of the Putah Creek alluvial fan tend to be sticky when wet and hard and rock-like when dry. They are easily worked only when the have a moderate moisture content. The early farmers working with draft animals kept a close watch on soil moisture so they could till when the ground was easily turned and the animals' labor would be most effective. For winter-growing crops, the soil was usually worked up late in the fall. There is almost always a few weeks of dry weather in November or December following the early rains when the moisture content of the soil is ideal for tillage. For summer growing crops, the ground was worked up in late spring, with the farmer closely watching the weather to catch the interval when the soil moisture was just right. Because tillage took place immediately prior to planting, the ground was bare only briefly.

Current farming practices are very different. Consider the case of a crop of tomatoes following a crop of wheat. The grain is harvested in July, and soon after the straw is cut and baled and taken from the field. The farmer then disks and cross-disks the field, followed by deep ripping at a depth of two feet or more—usually with three passes at three different angles. The field is disked twice more and then listed up into sixty inch beds. All of this work is done on utterly dry ground by heavy equipment working hard, shattering the hard soil and creating great plumes of dust in the process. If the winds are still, dust may hang in the air for days. This work is finished by August, and the field then sits bare for nine months. After the first rains, weeds will sprout (mostly spilled grains of wheat from the previous crop). The farmer sprays the field with an herbicide to kill the weeds, which turn an ominous orange color before they wither and die. The following April the beds are lightly harrowed, and the tomatoes are planted either by direct seeding or transplanting.

In nature, bare ground is an anomaly, to be seen only rarely, after a landslide or flood. Yet the field crop lands of the district are now bare a majority of the time. Fly over the region in October, and aside from orchards and vineyards, and a bit of pasture and alfalfa, all of the ground is plowed, and not a growing thing is to be seen. In part this way of working the land is made feasible by modern equipment. A three-hundred horsepower tractor does not care if the soil is wet or dry, and so the operator need not be canny about weather in the way that a farmer with mules must be. This allows the farmer of ten thousand acres of row crops to schedule the use of his equipment a year ahead of time. His expensive tractors can be worked twenty-four hours a day to earn their keep. The herbicides are the other half of the practice. By chemically killing all the winter-growing plants, the farmer saves himself some tillage in the spring, and the soil warms up a bit earlier, and so he can get his tomatoes in the ground a bit earlier.

One result of this practice is that the soil is missing a crop rotation. In the nine months that it sat bare through the rainy season it should have borne a cover crop, either deliberately planted or volunteering from whatever seeds are in the ground. Fifty years ago tomato ground always had a lush growth of chickweed and mustard and barley over the preceding winter. The winter crop maintains carbon levels (organic matter) in the soil, and sustains the soil microbes, worms, and arthropods. Bare ground through the rainy season, when the soil organisms should be active, makes for a very unhealthy soil. And the decrease in organic matter makes the ground more difficult to work.

FARM ECOLOGY 1: CYCLES OF MATTER

Garrison Keillor once remarked that farming is a spectator sport, and indeed, if one understands something of the rules of the game, the farm scene is endlessly interesting. But this is a complex business, not to be dispatched in just a few paragraphs. One approach, which leads in a roundabout way to an appreciation of the agrarian landscape, is to consider three cycles: matter, energy, and information.

It is instructive to draw a line around the perimeter of a farm and then to measure the movement of materials (or energy) across that line, onto and off the farm. In the case of matter, analysis usually is made for each chemical element, such as nitrogen, phosphorous, potassium and so forth. The conclusions reached depend very much on how one draws the line. For example, two adjacent farms, one producing grain which is sold to the other as feed for chickens, whose eggs are sold, might have very poor nitrogen economies when evaluated separately, but might be quite sound if the two were bundled together for the analysis. In the observations to follow I will sometimes consider cycles of matter for the entire region, and sometimes for individual crops.

Nitrogen is justifiably the most famous fertilizer. The cereal crops (wheat, rice, and corn) respond dramatically to added nitrogen; and other crops benefit as well. Nitrogen is abundantly present in the air, making up about 78% of the atmosphere, but it is in the form of nitrogen gas (N_2) which is inaccessible to plants. Atmospheric nitrogen can be converted to a form available to crops by microorganisms, of which nitrogen-fixing bacteria attached to roots of leguminous plants are most important. So one method of supplying the nitrogen needs of a farm is to grow nitrogen-fixing crops (vetch, beans, peas, clover), and plow them down into the soil where their decomposition will supply nitrogen to the crop that follows.

Figure 28. Walnut orchard underplanted with bell beans. Solano County

An alternative method of supplying nitrogen to crops is to use a nitrogen fertilizer. Typically this is manufactured using atmospheric nitrogen and natural gas as the raw materials; natural gas is also the source of energy to drive the transformation. The product is ammonia, which may be injected into the soil as anhydrous ammonia gas, or added to irrigation water, or solidified as a salt (ammonium sulfate) which can be applied at ground level by a tractor-pulled device or spread from an airplane.

The costs of supplying nitrogen from green manure crops is similar to the cost of purchased fertilizers. The legume crops may require more labor but less cash, and if weather is uncooperative they can interfere with farming operations to follow. The nitrogen fertilizers are sensitive to the price of natural gas, which is on the increase, whereas the cost of bean seed has been in decline. The farmer who is short of cash can let a portion of his bean crop go to seed and harvest it for his own use the following year, and so supply his crops with nitrogen with almost no cash outlay at all.

Aside from costs, there are good reasons to prefer green manure crops as a nitrogen source over chemical fertilizers. Natural gas is a limited resource, and the use of petroleum-based nitrogen fertilizers is not sustainable. Anhydrous ammonia is toxic, and when injected into the soil it kills soil organisms, including the beneficial ones. The legume crops, on the other hand, support a generous growth of beneficial soil microorganism which increases soil fertility and improves soil texture. Even a heavy, sticky soil will work up beautifully after a crop of bell beans. Despite the advantages of green manure crops as a nitrogen source, less than ten percent of the acreage in the district is planted to these crops in any given year.

In order to maintain a good level of soil nitrogen, the nitrogen removed with each harvest must be replaced with an equivalent of nitrogen taken from the atmosphere either by green manure crops or a fertilizer factory. Most crops grown in the district remove about 100-300 pounds of nitrogen per acre at harvest. The ability of the bean crops to fix nitrogen (100-200 pounds per acre) is such that they must be grown every year to maintain the balance of nitrogen; once every few years is not enough. In orchards, legume crops can be grown in winter when the trees are leafless (bell beans, crimson clover, and vetch are suitable winter bean crops). In farming systems where livestock are an integral part of the operation, things are different. If feedstuffs produced on the farm are fed to the livestock, and if the livestock manure is returned to the fields, then the only nitrogen leaving the farm is when the animal is sold. This is in the range of 15 to 30 pounds of nitrogen per acre per year, or only about one tenth the nitrogen loss from crops. So the relative scarcity of livestock in the region contributes to the high use of nitrogen fertilizers.

A decade or two hence this discussion might seem dated, for there is a possibility that through genetic engineering many crops could be made to fix nitrogen directly from the atmosphere, as do the beans and clovers. Although the economic and social dimensions of such a change are far from simple, at least in principle use of fossil fuels or green manure crops for fixing nitrogen could be greatly reduced.

Unlike nitrogen, phosphorous is not readily available in the atmosphere. Phosphate fertilizers are mined from geologic deposits of phosphate rock in Florida, Idaho, and Utah. The phosphorous (ground phosphate rock or super phosphate) is applied to the land at a much lower rate than nitrogen. Once the phosphorous has been spread onto fields, absorbed into growing crops which are harvested and fed to animals including humans, and finally dispersed into landfills, cemeteries, waterways and oceans, it cannot easily be concentrated again. And so even though elemental phosphorous is neither created nor destroyed, it nonetheless should be considered a nonrenewable resource. Much of the evidence of the necessity of phosphorous for plants is based on experiments in which the soil used is dead—either artificial soil in a greenhouse or in sterilized fields. This may give a false picture to the extent that in a healthy, living soil the abundant micro-organisms may mine phosphorous and convert it to a form available to crop plants,

Figure 29. A tank of anhydrous ammonia fertilizer, injected into irrigation water for corn. Solano County

whereas the same phosphorous in a sterile soil is chemically locked up and unavailable. There are well-managed, living soils that have produced excellent crops for more than a century without the addition of any phosphate fertilizers.

Calcium, another commonly used fertilizer in the district, may be spread at the rate of a ton or more per acre. Like phosphorous, the calcium is mined from geologic deposits, in this case deposits of gypsum (calcium sulfate) located in Southern California. In previous centuries, calcium and phosphorous were supplied to the land by spreading ground bones. In the alluvial fan of Putah Creek, with hardly any livestock, there is clearly an insufficiency of bones for fertilizer.

The most abundant element in harvested crops is carbon. When we consider a harvest of irrigated wheat (4,500 lbs/acre) or dry land wheat (2,500 lbs/acre) or almonds (3,000 lb/acre) or field corn (10,000 lb/acre) or alfalfa hay (13,000 lbs/acre), we are mostly measuring the weight of carbon. The district is a great exporter of carbon. Carbon is available in the atmosphere as carbon dioxide, at a low concentration (.03%), and this is captured by the growing crop through photosynthesis. It has long been known that the low level of carbon dioxide in the atmosphere is a limiting factor in the growth of many plants, and growers of greenhouse crops have for years been injecting carbon dioxide into their greenhouses to boost the productivity of their crops. Globally the level of carbon dioxide in the atmosphere is increasing as a result of burning fossil fuels; whether the associated pollution and climate change will undermine increased plant growth remains to be seen.

Carbon, as organic matter, is an important constituent of soils. It supports the activity of soil micro-organisms that are critical to the cycling of other minerals, and which also improve soil tilth. Throughout the twentieth century the carbon content of farm soils in North America has been decreasing, largely because of unwise farming practices. You can see this even from an airplane; soils in Iowa that once were black are now a washed-out tan color from loss of organic matter. High-carbon soils are friable and easily worked, and as a carbon is lost the soils become hard and difficult. The increasing energy required to till mineral soils has been largely masked by steadily increasing horsepower of farm tractors.

The loss of soil organic matter is not irreversible. Just a few seasons of growing green manure crops can largely restore it. But for the most part this is not being done. An example of a poor practice with respect to carbon management is seen in the harvest of wheat; after the grain is harvested, the remainder of the crop is baled as straw and sold off the farm. It would be better for the soil if the straw were plowed under. One cannot fault the farmer. Commodity prices are so low that sale of the grain may be a break-even proposition, with profit coming only from sale of the straw.

FARM ECOLOGY II: CYCLES OF ENERGY

Like matter, energy can neither be created nor destroyed, but unlike matter, which cycles endlessly, energy has a destiny. Its destiny (in a closed system) is to become heat. Nuclear energy in the sun becomes radiant energy reaching the earth. Some of this drives photosynthesis in plants (making chemical energy); some evaporates water from the oceans, which may precipitate on mountains as snow (gaining potential energy). As the snow melts and flows down hill it potential energy is converted to kinetic energy of flowing water, which may be channeled to run a turbine creating electrical energy. Fossil fuels are prehistoric solar energy captured by ancient plants and stored as chemical energy. And with each transformation, some energy is lost as heat.

Most of the energy used on a farm is radiant energy from the sun, which is used by plants to power the chemical work of photosynthesis. The efficiency of this process is very low. Overall, less than 3% of the solar energy is converted to plant growth. This reflects both the innate inefficiencies

Figure 30. The gear-head of an agricultural well can be driven by either a diesel motor (to the right) or an electric motor. It is relatively simple to switch from one power source to the other, and farmers closely watch the price of energy. Solano County

of plant chemistry and farming practices. By August, much of the land is bare ground, and with no crops there is no photosynthesis. This has partly to do with the mechanics of farming, and it also reflects the situation that farming in the district is water-limited rather than energy-limited.

The other major energy input to a farm is fossil fuel. One thinks of the big diesel tractors out plowing, but field operations account for roughly only a third of fossil fuel inputs. The pumping of water accounts for another third, and fertilizer (especially nitrogen fertilizers made from natural gas) account for the remaining third. Once the crop is harvested and out the farm gate, even greater amounts of fossil fuel are required in drying, shipping, and processing.

Figure 31. Harvesting safflower. Solano County

Crops are not equal in their use of fossil fuels. An orchard that is fertilized by a winter-grown green manure crop, and which requires very little in the way of tractor work, is a meager user of fossil fuel with the exception of pumping irrigation water. And the incident solar radiation is used throughout the year. A field crop such as corn, on the other hand, is a heavy user of fossil fuels. And if the corn is fed to cattle, which is a very inefficient chemical conversion, then the fossil-fuel requirement of the final product (beef) is extremely high. A pound of beef in the supermarket required more than a pound of fossil fuel to produce.

The heavy dependence on fossil fuels of farming in the district is obviously not sustainable; that is, petroleum is a non-renewable resource that will be notably scarcer within two decades, and when it is gone, alternatives will have to be found. Of course there was farming here before there were petroleum-driven devices, but it's productivity was considerably lower than modern farming. Not only was a third of the acreage required to maintain horses and mules, but in the absence of irrigation and fertilizer, production on the remaining land was also much lower than modern production. Although there are appealing aspects to returning to a horse-based farming system, it would require a revolution in agriculture. A moderate size tractor has the power output of eighty horses plus two-hundred men; where would these horses and men come from? A more likely alternative is the use of crop-based fuels. In particular, vegetable oils can be used in place of diesel fuel for both field operations and pumping of water. Safflower and canola are winter-grown, non-irrigated crops, producing a clean-burning diesel-fuel equivalent of about 100 gallons per acre. Less than ten percent of the land devoted to these crops could supply all the farming energy needs of the district. The region could become self-sufficient in farm energy with almost no notable change in the landscape.

INFORMATION

Unlike matter and energy, information can be created, and it can be destroyed. The extinction of a species, or of a culture, represents irremediable loss of information, just as the creation of a work of art is growth of information. We have inklings from genetics and cybernetics about how information works, but this is a science still awaiting its Newton and its Einstein.

On a farm, information is embedded in the genomes of the crops being grown, and in the instinctive and learned habits of the many organisms that interact with the crop, (pollinators, pests, disease organisms, beneficial organisms), and in the mind of the farmer. In the twentieth century there was a great movement to simplify the information content of farming. Monocultures of genetically uniform crops were esteemed, and the unofficial motto of farm management might have been 'Kill everything except the crop.' This is the industrial approach to farming.

An alternative approach adopts a motto from ecology: 'Diversity creates stability.' In this view, the health of the farm correlates with its informational complexity. A diversity of organisms and habitats makes for a stable and healthy farm. Complex systems (salt marshes, coral reefs, rain forests) are remarkably able to recover from perturbation, whereas monocultures are prone to catastrophic failures.

In order to talk about monoculture, we first have to identify the size of plots we are considering. To a caterpillar walking on the ground, six tomato plants in a row represents a monoculture. But to a butterfly on a windy day, forty-acre plots are a polyculture. In may make most sense to consider the district as a whole. If there are eight thousand acres of wheat in the district, and it is all the same variety, then how it is divided up into fields is not really relevant—it is a monoculture. How did it come to pass that we have only one commercial variety of wheat? In part this has to do with the requirements of mechanical harvesting: a crop that is very uniform in height and in timing of maturity makes for an easier and more efficient harvest. But the demand for uniformity in the wheat crop extends far beyond the harvest. The mills, and bakers, and brewers, and other users of wheat require an absolutely consistent product so that their industrial processing can be completely predictable without requiring any day-to-day human judgment. And the processors in turn point to the consumers, who want their product to taste exactly the same every time they buy it. A beer that varies in taste from batch to batch will not be popular. And so we have only the one variety of wheat.

In primitive farming systems a genetically very diverse wheat crop is sown. What part of the crop reaches maturity and is harvested depends on how well it is adapted to the local climate, and diseases, and farming practices, and on the peculiarities of that particular year. And each place is a little different, and each year is a little different, and so over many generations thousands of local races of wheat have evolved, each particularly well adapted to its place. We would have a healthier farm ecosystem if we followed similar practices and sowed diverse open-pollinated seed of local origin, but the crop would not find a buyer in our markets. An increase in complexity of biological information in the crop requires simultaneously changes in the social institutions involved in processing, marketing, and consumption of what is harvested.

Instead of increasing the informational complexity of a farm by growing genetically diversified crops in preference to monocultures, farmers in the district have created diversity by promoting a variety of habitats, particularly along the farm edges. Hedgerows, strips of perennial meadow, shallow ponds, and diversified road-side and ditch-side plantings provide habitat for a great many organisms that can in turn interact with the cultivated parts of the farm. This works well for vertebrates and the more mobile arthropods, and is certainly superior to the sterility that seemed to be the goal of conventional farming in the 1980's. But it does little to prevent epidemics of crop disease, for example, that could be forestalled by using a genetically diverse crop.

ORGANIC FARMING

Only a small part of the acreage in the district is farmed organically, and as a variable in the landscape its role is modest. But if the organic farms occupy only small area, they occupy a large space in the public imagination, and therefore merit some comments.

The initial notion behind organic farming was simple enough: the organic farmers wanted to farm in a way that was environmentally beneficent, and to produce a crop untainted by poisons. To give the word 'organic' a consistent meaning, a formal definition was required. Farming is an extremely complex undertaking, and commissions charged with formulating rules and definitions for organic farming found, after twenty years of bickering, that dogma is much easier than reason. The result is an arbitrary and capricious set of rules making up the legal definition of organic farming, enforced by a policing bureaucracy. These rules often run contrary to common sense, and force illogical practices on the organic farmer, who is justifiably frustrated by them. But there is a great deal of money at stake, which makes change difficult.

Figure 32. Apple orchard farmed organically. The abundant weeds do not harm the trees, but they preclude the use of micro-sprinkler irrigation, so that furrow irrigation, more wasteful of water and of energy, is required. Weed seeds blowing onto adjacent properties put a management burden on neighboring farms, especially if crops of agronomic seeds are being grown. Solano County

As a landscape element, organic farms differ little from other farms much of the year. You can see the farmer out in January spraying his orchard with fungicides, and have no way of telling if the farm is organic or not. Probably the main difference is an abundance of weeds on the organic farms. The menu of pesticides permitted to organic farmers does not include an effective herbicide, and so the organic farmer either increases cultivation, (using more fossil fuel than a conventional farm), or lets the weeds go.

Figure 33. Empty pesticide containers. Yolo County

There are some who benefit by promoting the notion that there are only two kinds of farming: organic and conventional. That dichotomy is false. There are thousands of farming systems in use, and each farmer does things a little differently. There are many intelligent and thoughtful farmers who have a good grasp of ecology and who have invented sound farming systems that are appropriate for their land and their markets, but which do not fit the narrow definition of organic. Within the farming district of the Putah Creek alluvial fan, I estimate that between a quarter and a third of the land is farmed with a system which is neither conventional nor organic. The orchardists in particular have developed many innovative practices to reduce the use of chemicals and increase the ecological diversity and health of their farms. A locally based program (BIOS—Biologically Integrated Orchard Systems) has been very effective in promoting a shift toward sustainable practices as an alternative to more chemically intensive methods. And I see the rising price of chemical inputs and the falling value of commodities as favoring a movement of more farmers from conventional to other farming systems, including organic farming.

An enthusiast might think, 'Wouldn't it be wonderful if all the farms in the district were organic.' This is unlikely to happen, and the organic farmers themselves would probably be opposed. Economically, organic farming can survive only as a minority movement. A hefty price premium for the organic label is what makes organic farming feasible. As more and more acreage is converted to organic registration, that price premium melts away and the prices slump back toward standard commodity prices. At the organic farming conferences one hears a steady whine from the organic growers that 'Agribusiness is co-opting our movement.' What they're talking about is dollars. As an ecology-minded citizen the organic farmer wishes that all farms were organic, but as a businessman he wants to be the only one.

The organic farmers are correct on one point: among conventional farmers there is occasionally some very bad farming going on. I was once driving down a back road in Solano county, studying the countryside, and up ahead I could see a field of a crop with silver foliage. I thought from the color and texture it must be watermelons, but the field was at least 160 acres, far bigger than the normal melon patch in this region. As I got closer, I saw that the field was tomatoes, and that it had been dusted so heavily with powdered fungicides that it looked as if half an inch of snow had fallen. I parked my truck and got out. Across the road, sixty feet away, was another tomato field, at the same stage of maturity, that had not been sprayed. I walked around in both fields looking at the crop. They both had a bit of mildew here and there, as tomatoes always do, but the incidence of diseased fruit was about the same in both the dusted and the unsprayed field. What desperate wrong-headedness could have lead to dumping thousands of pound of pesticide per acre on the one field, probably unnecessarily? I suspect absentee corporate owners with inattentive management, but that is just speculation.

WHAT SHOULD A GOOD FARM LOOK LIKE?

The question of what makes a good farm—one that is ecologically and economically sound, and socially just—has been much considered for the valleys of Kentucky and Ohio (Wendell Berry, Louis Bromfield) and for the plains of Kansas (Gene Logdsdon), and for southern Japan (Masanobu Fukuoka). But their conclusions do not apply so readily to the Putah Creek alluvial fan, where the climate and topography are different, and the crops are different, and the markets are different. Even the question is probably inappropriate. Instead of asking, 'what should a good farm look like?' we should be asking 'what should a good agrarian landscape look like?' (In considering this question I will accept as given the population density of the district and the standard of living of the inhabitants, although I think it would be better if both of those were reduced by half.)

Wendell Berry has proposed that the criterion for measuring an agrarian landscape should be health, rather than wealth. The well-ordered landscape has healthy soil, healthy crops, healthy people, and a healthy society. In this, farming is akin to doctoring. To be sure, dollars are involved, but only incidentally. But certain entrepreneurs have mistaken the tail for the dog, and have transformed the health care industry and agribusiness into enterprises based on the dollar, to the grief of doctors and their patients, and farmers, and the land.

Figure 34. Sweet corn destined for a supermarket chain. The crop duster sprays toxic insecticides every 96 hours to ensure a worm-free crop. Solano County

Healthy soil is soil that has a high respiratory rate. This can be thought of as the collective breathing of all the underground organisms—bacteria, fungi, algae, worms, arthropods, reptiles, mammals, and the roots of plants. A soil which is dry, or cold, or heavily compacted, or toxic, or sterile, will have a low respiratory rate, whereas a soil that is well aerated, moist, warm, full of organic matter, and full of organisms will have a high rate of respiration. By this measure, the average health of farm soils in the district has declined during the twentieth century.

The practice most responsible for declining health of the soil is the overuse of pesticides, especially herbicides. The wholesale killing off of plant life devitalizes the soil, endangers water conservation, and weakens the biologic health of the region. Alternatives are already available and well known; economic incentives need to be rigged to favor them. Equally problematic is excessive tillage. Tilling a field disrupts the structure of the soil, dries out the ground, and smashes many

Figure 35. Bins of walnuts, destined for export throughout the world. Yolo County

small creatures in the process. We can take density of earthworms as a simple measure of soil health. A field that is tilled twice a year has no earthworms in it, and yet in a nearby fencerow, outside the path of tillage, worms are numerous. In other districts, no-till and minimum-till farming have been shown to provide numerous benefits for both the farmer and the soil, but these techniques have been little tried in this district. As a hypothetical example, following harvest of wheat, the straw could be rolled rather than cut and baled, and a crop of crimson clover drilled into the stubble. The clover is irrigated up in October and allowed to grow through the winter. The following spring the clover would be mowed to ground level with a flail mower, and tomato transplants could be set with strip tillage. Undoubtedly there would be technical problems to be worked out with such an approach, but it would surely result in a healthier soil than severe tillage followed by nine months of bare ground between wheat harvest and tomato planting, which is what we have now.

One trait of a healthy agrarian landscape is that the local farm economy supplies the agricultural needs of the local communities. Almost every kind of crop can be grown in the district: fruits, vegetables, grains, nuts, oil seeds, timber, cotton, wool, livestock, poultry, herbs, flowers, berries, and fish. By this standard, the district is only partially successful. Rather than having eggs reach our district from three hundred miles away, it would be more appropriate to have eggs raised locally from hens fed on locally grown grain. And instead of having milk shipped from even greater distances, it would be better to have a few small dairies locally, even if the milk costs more by a few cents per gallon. One benefit of this is a decreased dependence on fossil fuels and a decrease in the number of trucks on the road. Also, carbon, nitrogen, and other nutrients are kept within the district rather than exported, as with hay sent to distant dairies. More important, local production builds the sense of community. School children visit the dairy, they understand where their milk comes from, they feel social connection to the dairyman and his family, which may include some of their classmates.

The development of a local food-and-fiber economy (which is contrary to the historic trend of the last two hundred years) requires more than just a change in the farm scene. It also requires adaptation by processors and handlers, that is, the dairies, the canneries, the cotton gins, the flour mills, and so forth. Consider the example of wheat, a common crop in the district. Only one variety of wheat is grown commercially here, a type of red wheat destined to be made into flour for cakes and cookies. Noncommercially, more than a thousand varieties of wheat are grown in the district, as part of the germplasm collection at the University of California. Most of these wheats grow well. There is no good agronomic reason why we could not grow the types of wheat suited for making bread or pasta or beer or any of the dozens of other uses of wheat around the world, instead of importing wheat from the Dakotas or Australia or the Ukraine. But to do this requires a flour mill that is adaptable to milling a number of kinds of wheat into a great variety of products, often in small batches. Similarly, a local economy would require canneries and frozen food packers set up to handle a variety of crops made into an even greater variety of products.

Supplying local needs would require less than twenty per cent of the land in the district. Putting another eight to ten percent into oil seed crops for conversion to diesel fuel could supply the on-farm energy needs of the district. Much of the rest would best be devoted to orchards. There are only a few places in the world where walnuts, almonds, and prunes can be happily grown, and this is one of them. The products of local orchards are shipped throughout the Americas, Europe, and the Pacific Rim. The orchards are the global connection for the district. (In fairness, canned tomatoes also are shipped throughout the world, with the Great Valley accounting for forty percent of the world output). There is another good reason for putting much of the land into orchards. Orchards, when managed well, are ecologically far more benign than field and row crops. If a

Figure 36. Old orchard logs (walnut) are sawn into valuable lumber. Solano County

winter green-manure crop is under planted as a nitrogen source, then the fossil fuel inputs are very low. The ground is not left barren nor is it disturbed by frequent tillage, good use is made of incoming sunlight, and the trees provide habitat for wildlife throughout the year. And when orchards are allowed to reach an old age, the trees (walnuts and almonds, at least) can be sawn into valuable lumber. Moreover, the labor requirements of orchards are spread evenly throughout the year, which favors a stable labor force rather than the seasonal hiring of itinerant crews.

Conversely, corn is probably the crop least defensibly grown in the district. It is a tremendous user of water, soil nutrients, and fossil fuels, and its conversion to beef is energetically very inefficient. Measured in dollars, corn is profitable because the markets are manipulated by government subsidies and because it relies on cheap fossil fuel, which is subsidized by environmental degradation and bad foreign policies. But in an ecological currency corn is highly unprofitable. Raising corn for conversion to ethanol as a gasoline substitute is also inappropriate; corn culture is ecologically unsound, and ethanol is a weak fuel with only seventy percent of the energy density of gasoline. In contrast, oil seeds crops grown over winter are ecologically well adapted to the district, and their oils have about ninety percent of the energy density of diesel fuel. If we are to have crop-based fuel, biodiesel makes far more sense than ethanol.

Farming can coexist with, and benefit from, a diverse ecosystem. There has been much interest in the district in establishing and maintaining hedgerows along farm edges (another anti-historic trend). Maintenance of the Putah Creek riparian corridor, and establishment of perpendicular branch corridors based on hedgerows and occasional ponds, would do much to foster wildlife diversity in the district while requiring a relatively small commitment of land. One of the most stringent limitations on vertebrates in the district is not lack of food, but lack of nesting sites. Construction and placement of nesting boxes is a simple and inexpensive measure to promote wildlife. One walnut farmer I know has put up enough bat boxes to attract large bat colonies, and the bats control the insect pests of the walnuts. He has not had to use insecticides in several years.

One could make a case that there are too few animals in the district. Almost every ecologically sound farming system includes an abundance of livestock. Poultry (chickens, turkeys, geese, and ducks) could be added to both row crop and orchard farms. One farmer in a neighboring district ranges turkeys under olive trees, fattening them on the fallen fruit. The mechanical harvest of prunes leaves ten percent or more of the crop on the ground, which could be foraged by pigs. Fish culture (including crayfish) could be integrated into the irrigation cycles of many farms. Raising cattle for beef is untenable in the district—it uses too much water and fossil fuels for the product. It is no accident that cattle culture in the US is concentrated in the wettest region—East Texas, Louisiana, Mississippi, and Florida. It is logical to support a small dairy or two in the district. (Although I believe that the food pyramid taught in our schools, which ranks dairy products as a critical feature of a good diet, is a suspicious document. It is produced not by the National Institute of Health, but by the Department of Agriculture, which is a partisan of the dairy industry.)

From the social and economic perspectives it would be best to see family sized farms of not more than a few hundred acres, as well as specialty farms of only a dozen or twenty acres. It takes years to become familiar with the idiosyncrasies of a piece of land, and it is better farmed by one observant individual of long tenure than by a distant corporation with a constantly changing staff.

There is another aspect of farming in the district that is subtle but disturbing, and that is the absence of young farmers. Nearly all the farmers are older than fifty, and the median age is well above fifty-five. Who is going to take over when they retire? There is no shortage of young people wishing to farm. But land is so expensive that for a young person to buy a forty acre plot of good soil, and put in an ag well, and buy the minimum equipment needed to farm it, requires well over half a million dollars. The young farmers don't have that kind of money (and if they did, they would get a better return from buying bonds than from farming). What they can afford is a patch of class three soil back in the hills that will always be a heartbreak to farm. We need new social institutions that allow the young farmer to have long-term use of the good land in the district without the need to put up tremendous amounts of capital.

THE RURAL LANDSCAPE AS AN URBAN AMENITY

The rural landscape of the Putah Creek alluvial fan between Davis and Winters is exceptionally handsome. The farms are well-kept and prosperous, the harvests abundant, and the rural working people purposeful and productive. Not a single billboard defaces the landscape; the county governments have been vigilant in preventing this kind of pollution (or perhaps there are too few travelers to attract advertisers). To people who live in town, a knowledge their surroundings forms an important part of their sense of where they are in the world. Some run or bike into the countryside daily to renew their spirits; others may venture out only once a year, and yet the sense of their surroundings, though subconscious, is always there.

When I was a child there was a shortage of farm labor in the region, and my sister and I used to earn some pocket money by picking tomatoes in the fields around Davis and pitting apricots for the fruit-drying yards in Winters. The result of this was more than just a few dollars in our pockets, welcome enough in those lean times; we also felt proud. We were part of a great and wonderful enterprise—farming. Townspeople today are not engaged with the countryside in this way—they are mostly spectators.

There is obvious merit in reconnecting urban people to farms, which would make them partisans of farming and powerful allies in the preservation of the rural landscape. I have been entertaining the notion of starting a labor cooperative, specifically one devoted to olive oil. Olive trees grow happily in the district, even without irrigation, and their product, olive oil, is one of the most healthful and enjoyable of foods. But the olive oil industry has never thrived here because of the expense of the hand labor involved in picking the fruit. I would like to see a large-scale planting of olive trees in the district—orchards, field borders, and avenues, in conjunction with the formation of olive-oil cooperatives made up of townspeople. At harvest time, in the fall and winter, people from the town would come to the countryside and pick the olives, and be paid in olive oil. Most townspeople are well off, and have no need of a few extra dollars. Their motivation would be the primal satisfaction of harvesting their own food, and the congeniality of an occasional day spent working in the country with their families and friends. A portion of the oil would be distributed to the members of the cooperative according to how much fruit they picked, and the rest would be sold to support the farmer, the pressman, and the bottler. This would foster an engagement of town people with the countryside, both in the harvesting of the fruit and in the enjoyment of the oil. For people who work at abstract occupations, labor at the olive harvest could be profoundly satisfying. And I believe that by having a tangible stake in the countryside, the townspeople would become very protective of the rural landscape. I have mentioned this notion to a number of people; nine out of ten tell me it will never work, but the tenth one says, 'That sounds great. Where can I sign up?' On the strength of that ten percent I have planted twelve hundred olive trees for a little trial.

There is an odd notion entrenched in our culture that simple labors—gathering and preparing one's food, cleaning one's house, mending one's clothes, or walking a few miles to a destination—are drudgery that should be avoided by delegating these tasks to machines or to persons of foreign birth. This is supposed to create more free time that can be used for shopping and watching television, that is, frivolity and alienation. Many people have lost sight of the truth that these simple daily tasks, carried out in an unhurried way, are a form of spiritual practice. I suspect that the townsman who comes to the country to pick olives, expecting only a bucolic holiday, may be surprised to discover the spiritual dimension of that simple labor. *Labore orare est.*

Figure 37. Cucumber seed harvester. Yolo County

Figure 38. Bean harvester at work. Solano County

Chapter Eight:

Machines

> **Wholly aside from the value of a tool as an implement of tillage and as a weapon for the pursuit of weeds is its merit merely as a shapely and interesting instrument.**
>
> L.H. Bailey, *Manual of Gardening*, 1914

Like an animal, a machine is a nexus of complexity and unpredictability, and so it commands our attention disproportionately to its size in the landscape. A farm machine working a field is always of interest, with its rhythmic noises, and smoke, and movement, and steady transformation of the landscape. Machines are agents of landscaping in the literal sense, i.e. shaping the land, as they rearrange the earth and its vegetation. What was this morning a field of ten-foot-tall corn is by afternoon a field of waist-high broken stalks, and by evening, with the passage of a flail mower, this is reduced to an ankle-deep litter of cobs and shreds. In the next few days the ground is disked, cross-disked, ripped, cross-ripped, disked again, and listed into tall thirty inch beds for a crop of onions to follow, the landscape transformed from the field of tall corn to a corrugated plane of bare earth in just a few days.

Most of the tillage machines are brutally simple, but harvesters are ingenious, improbable descendents of 1930s' science fiction. A tomato harvester lumbers through the field and a river of tomatoes pours from its conveyer, filling a twenty-ton bin in a few minutes. Bean harvesters, cotton pickers, vine-seed harvesters, and nut sweepers, when deeply considered, are astounding artifacts, and such a machine at work is an engaging feature of the rural landscape. The earliest of these to find success in California was the grain combine, which performs two functions (reaping and threshing), hence the name 'combine'. Although invented in the east (the first patent, in 1828, was from the state of Maine), combines first succeeded in the Great Valley of California. The hot dry summers provided two essential features for success: the dry ground was firm enough that heavy machinery could move over it without risk of miring in boggy spots, and the grain was dry enough that threshing could immediately follow reaping without having to leave the cut grain in the field to dry for a few weeks, as was done in the east. Early combines, either horse drawn or self-propelled, were the basis of the district's success in wheat culture in the last quarter of the nineteenth century.

THE SIZE OF FARM MACHINES

The earliest farm machines in the district were behemoths. The steam engines that provided motive power were massive, and the rest of the tractor was built to the same scale. A railroad locomotive unconfined to its tracks is the general idea. Some of the early combines weighed twenty tons, had wheels eight-feet in diameter, and cut a swath forty feet wide. Such machines were built locally in the valley, and the city of Stockton became a center for manufacture of farm machinery. Its most famous company, the Holt Co., developed track-laying tractors, at first powered by steam, then gasoline, then diesel. In 1925, Holt combined with the Best company of San Leandro to form the famous Caterpillar Tractor Company.

The enormous machines of the steam era were not suited to the small farm. Their great expense required them to work at least a few thousand acres to justify their purchase, and so they were to be found only on the biggest farms. But by the 1920's the nature of tractor manufacturing changed. Many small and inexpensive tractors in the range of twenty to fifty horsepower became available, and these were well suited to the smaller orchard, row-crop, vineyard, and mixed farms that typified the district at that time. With the proper implements these tractors could not only be used for tillage and cultivation, but could also pump water, saw wood, grind grain, generate electricity, spread manure, haul hay, deliver produce to the rail depot, and perform a number of other tasks around the farm.

After 1950, the trend toward smaller tractors was reversed. Each year new models, bigger and more powerful, were introduced until by the 1980's tractors were being built as big as the old steam monsters from a hundred years before, albeit far more powerful for their size. We now have tractors of more than four hundred horsepower capable of pulling a twenty-four foot wide disk plow at a speed of sixteen miles per hour.

TRACTOR SIZE AND FARM SIZE

It is a truism that farm machines are designed and built to suit the needs of farmers. But it is equally true that farms have evolved so as to fit the abilities of the machines that are available.

Machinery is an agent of rural landscaping not only the obvious sense that the machines regularly work the crops and soil surface, but also in a more subtle way in which they influence the nature of farming as an enterprise.

A farmer decides to buy a new tractor, twice as powerful (and more than twice as expensive) as his old one. The rationale is that one man can plow twice as many acres in the course of a day, and therefore the per-acre cost of labor is diminished. But if the plowing is done in half the time, then the tractor sits idle in its shed, and the capital invested in it is not working. So the farmer leases some more land in the neighborhood to keep the tractor busy; now he's farming twelve hundred acres instead of five hundred. And when he goes to buy his next tractor, he again buys one twice the size, for the same reasons he did last time. There are other reasons, too: he's fallen in love with the big tractor; it gives him status among his peers, and increases his own estimation of himself. And the bigger tractor can work dry ground. Soils in the district, when dry, are like concrete, and require great power for tillage. After the first heavy rain of fall the ground is muddy, and the clay soils are sticky and unworkable. But as the soil gradually dries out a stage is reached where the moisture content is perfect for tillage; the ground is like cake, springy and moist and full of air. That is when it can be worked easily. The old farmers tilling with mules or a small tractor waited until mid or late fall when almost always there is a suitable interval to get in and prepare the fields and plant the fall crops when the soil can be worked with light equipment. But the man farming five thousand acres on credit cannot take chances with the weather, so he buys the big equipment that can work the dry ground. All through the late summer and fall the tractors work around the clock, ripping to a depth of thirty inches, disking and cross-disking, and listing up beds, getting ready for fall planting, or even the plantings of next spring. Through the night the rural resident hears the big tractors groaning as they strain at their labors, and dust from pulverized dry earth coats the countryside.

Figure 39. Plowing dry ground in August. Solano County

Figure 40. Mechanical prune harvester at work. Solano County

This is not to suggest that big tractors are the only reason, or even the major reason, for big farms. But they are a factor. A two-hundred-thousand dollar tractor bought on credit has to work around the clock to earn its keep. The result is a farm of five thousand acres or more, of which there are several in the district.

A farm of five thousand acres is a fundamentally different enterprise than a farm of five hundred acres. The big farm is a corporation with a large payroll of salaried employees, and the farmer himself, if there is one, is more likely to be found in an office than walking his fields. The big farm embodies the metaphor that agriculture is an industry, simply a form of manufacturing, a metaphor much encouraged by the equipment manufacturers, fertilizer and pesticide dealers, petroleum vendors, and the Department of Agriculture. The nature of big farming affects the landscape in three ways.

I have already mentioned that the big farming operations work the ground dry immediately after harvest. The result is that much of the countryside is bare earth for a good part of the year. Tomato beds to planted in April are already prepared the preceding July as soon as the wheat is harvested. Except for orchards and alfalfa fields, and perhaps some late rice, the country seen from the air in October is a patchwork of rectangles of brown bare earth.

The big farms uniformly follow a certain style of farming. Farms of five thousand acres and more are usually financed by a bank, and bankers are notorious for their fear of the unconventional. So the banker, concerned to protect his capital, insists that the farmer hire a pest control advisor. The advisor figures that his job is to bring in a clean crop at all costs, so he recommends a heavy hand with the chemicals. The fields on the big farms are remarkably free of weeds and pests. Hybrid seeds are used that produce a crop of perfect uniformity. The fields look like illustrations from a textbook. No innovative management is to be expected here. This is farming by the book, which is to say, the agribusiness book. In contrast, on a little family farm of a few hundred acres one may expect to find innovations of various kinds: hedgerows, owl boxes, unorthodox crop rotations, unusual equipment, experimental cover crops. The orchardists in particular are independent and inventive in their management. The smallest farms of all, the little specialty truck farms of a dozen acres which supply the fruit stands and farmers markets, are most inventive of all. I do not know of any that are farmed conventionally.

The third feature of big farming that affects the landscape is the peoplelessness of it. Here is a six

Figure 41. Tomato harvester. Yolo County

hundred acre field of alfalfa and no one is to be seen—no worker, no house. The irrigation is automated, the hay is cut by a mobile crew, a week later it is baled at night, and it is gathered and hauled the next morning. You could watch the field every day for a year and never say, 'Ah, there's the farmer.'

There used to be a burned out farmstead on road 31. A few charred timbers and rusted pipes stood over the old foundation, and a thicket of feral rose bushes covered what had once been the yard. In the remains of the garage sat the burnt hulk of a '53 Cadillac, its chromium dental work grinning through the brambles. One day men showed up with heavy machinery—loaders and excavators and trucks—and they scooped up all the remains of the homestead—foundations, Cadillac, roses, and all—and hauled it away. By the next season the site was incorporated into the adjacent field, with no evidence left that there had ever been a home there. This is a landscape feature of the big farms—the farm without a farmstead and without a farmer.

STEEL ON THE FARM

There are farmers who never throw anything away. When a piece of machinery comes to the end of its useful life, they drag it to a hedgerow and leave it to rust. I have studied a couple of such farms, making an inventory of the equipment, both active and retired, and calculating its weight. The estimate is a crude one, but I reckon about eleven hundred pounds of steel per acre farmed. On my own place, counting only the active equipment, there is about eight hundred pounds of steel per acre farmed. Added up over tens of thousands of acres, this represents a staggering movement of iron to the district from the steel mills of the Midwest.

Why does the farmer need all this steel? Each year in the winter there are farm shows where the manufacturers of farm equipment display their products. The equipment is shiny and full of promise, and the salesmen are affable, and the farmer is tempted to buy a new device with the hope that it will solve an old problem. Usually the problem is not so easily fixed. The buying of farm equipment has something in common with the buying of lottery tickets: much of what you get for your money is the fantasy that life is suddenly going to become easier. So part of the equipment in the farmer's shed is a collection of steel lottery tickets. Other pieces are indeed truly useful under conditions that occur only rarely. A particular type of harrow may be needed only once in three years, but when the farmer needs it, he needs it today, and there is no possibility of renting one because all of his neighbors are in the same boat. And so implements accumulate for those rare occasions when one needs them. Nut harvesting machinery is somewhat like this. Nut harvest may last only ten days; the rest of the year the equipment gathers dust. When the day comes that conditions are right to start the harvest, the farmer has to move speedily, for timeliness is critical. If a storm is brewing in the Gulf of Alaska, headed this way, the harvest races on all day and through the night. And the harvest period is the same for everyone—there is no possibility of sharing equipment with a neighbor, or checking it out from a co-op.

THE SOUNDS OF MACHINES

Although machines are powerful agents in the manipulation of the visible landscape, when we consider the *experience* of landscape, this is not their most important role. Rather, it is their sound. There is an aesthetics of engine sounds. The Italians like their cars tuned to a high, strained, pitch, like a tenor whose trousers are too tight. The Americans prefer a car with low growl. In motorcycles, the Japanese favor the sound of an enraged mosquito, whereas the Harley-Davidson, whose sound is its soul, produces a rapid-fire string of insolent farts as frankly rebellious as the tattoos, greasy ponytails, and extended middle fingers of the drivers. Some big diesels idle at a slow bass so deep it is almost felt rather than heard; it is a comforting sound, like the steady breathing of a Percheron.

I once tried for several days to make a tape recording of some bird songs, and found I could not do it without the sounds of an internal combustion engine in accompaniment. Engine noise is a constant feature of the rural district for most of the year. Farm equipment works around the clock seven days a week; there is no holy hour, no Sabbath. And yet, it is not tractors, nor the

Figure 42. Not all of the ingenious machines have been invented yet. Hand-harvesting onion seed. Yolo County

occasional automobile, that has so degraded the rural soundscape. It is airplanes. It is not difficult to walk yourself out of ear shot of road traffic, but there is no escaping the noise of planes, beaming from overhead. A small plane can be heard over an area of forty-thousand acres, and in the district there are enough small planes that the sound is nearly continuous. At Stevenson Bridge, some thirty planes per hour cross Putah Creek on a weekend. These are not thirty different planes, but just the same few, flying up and down the creek, or around in circles. And a dozen or so crossings per hour are skydiving planes from Yolo County airport.

Skydiving in Yolo County may be considered environmental vandalism equal to jet skis in Lake Tahoe (now illegal) and snowmobiles in national parks (now illegal). The jet skis and snowmobiles were outlawed because their redeeming social value (none) could not justify their degradation of an obviously special landscape. But in the district the value of the rural landscape is subtle, and so it is not protected. If it were the eye being offended rather than the ear, if this were trash being strewn over eighty thousand acres rather than noise, people would go to jail for it. But our society seems to have decided that the ear is not privileged, and that the soundscape may be freely desecrated. Blind people know about this.

I was once talking to a neighbor about the need for us to organize and take political action against garbage air traffic, such as skydiving. 'What planes?' he asked. He had to shout to be heard over the roar of a plane that was directly overhead. 'What planes?' I had to laugh. Some people have learned to edit out noise in their environment. In the complicated passage from sensation to perception the noise is shunted away. But it seems to me that this is a little increment of suicide. In not hearing what one hears, one chooses to be less than alert, less than fully awake, a little bit dead. During the decade when I was in my twenties I worked on a botanical survey in the remotest parts of the western Amazon. There were no engines to be heard there, or other extraneous noises. Every sound was meaningful, and I learned to be attentive. A good trait in the forest; a bad trait for modern California. I regard our soundscape with despair. It seems that in the steady decline of the global sound space toward a cacophony of roaring engines, barking dogs, sirens, and gunfire, we are already well along the path.

Figure 43. Classic farmstead: house, tank tower, windmill, and barn. Yolo County

Chapter Nine:

Rural Buildings

> **True barn.**
> **True temple.**
> **There is no difference.**
> **Nowadays we think there is a great difference between a barn and a temple, but this is true only when either is built (as it usually is) with the assumption that there should be a difference.**
>
> John Townsend, Jr., 'Looking for the simple life,' in *Whole Earth Review*, Fall 1987, p. 94

The traditional rural homestead of the nineteenth century included four essential elements: the house, the barn, the tank tower, and the windmill. To these might be added a miscellany of smaller out-buildings: a smithy, a kennel, a poultry coop, a packing shed, a privy, an outdoor kitchen, and perhaps a dormitory for seasonal workers. In part because of the danger of fire, the buildings were usually widely spaced, with the homestead occupying as much as an acre of ground. A canopy of trees—native walnuts and oaks, or elms and maples brought from the east—shaded the homestead.

THE HOUSE

There are several dozen fine nineteenth-century houses in the district. What one might notice first is their size: these are big buildings or four or five thousand square feet. Ceilings of twelve to sixteen feet high, which helped cool the interior in summer, make for a tall two-story house. A prosperous farm needed a house this big. Families were large, and often were augmented by guests. Passage on muddy roads in winter was a slow business, and travelers would be put up for the night in farmhouses that served as seasonal hotels. The house also served for schooling, musical performances, dances, and religious services, and for conducting the business of the farm. One fine old house in the district, in Yolo County, has a second-floor ballroom with a false floor mounted on springs.

A house has a front, a back, and two sides; we speak of it 'facing' the road. Old rural houses in the district were generally oriented square to the road, but with no regard to the cardinal directions. Whether a house faced east, west, north, or south depended only on it position in relation to the nearest road, with little account made for orientation to the sun or prevailing winds.

The architectural styles of rural houses in the district are national styles, reflecting whatever was current in Sacramento or San Francisco, or what was to be seen in the magazines. Surviving houses from the nineteenth century are in the Greek revival, or Italianate, or Queen Anne styles. In the first half of the twentieth century we find shingle style and craftsman bungalows, as well as a nondescript style that might be called 'simple cottage.' The simple cottage is a modest wooden structure with a gabled roof of five:twelve or six:twelve pitch, double hung windows, and a small porch in front and another in back. The house is devoid of ornamentation beyond the rhythm of the placement of windows and doors. It is equally to be found in town and in the country, in either place serving as a generic house of the era. After World War II modern ranch style houses became common in the countryside. They sat low to the ground, with a concrete slab foundation rather than a raised floor, and with ceilings dropped to only eight feet to accommodate the four-by-eight foot size of sheet goods (plywood and drywall) that developed after the war. (I believe that adopting the four-by-eight foot size as standard was a blunder; three-by-nine sheets would make for less claustrophobic rooms and would be easier for workers to handle).

Figure 44. Nineteenth century rural house. Yolo County

No local vernacular architectural style ever developed in the district, as it did in a similar era and climate in New South Wales, for example. The prevailing styles have always been the styles of town, transposed to the countryside, where they were not especially well suited to the climate. A low house with an encircling veranda in a style well known to Australia or India would be appropriate here; the veranda keeps the house cool in summer, and fends off wet weather in winter. Only a few houses of this type are found in the district, and those are fairly recent.

Figure 45. Nineteenth century farmstead. Yolo County

Uniformly old houses in the district are built of wood. Even foundations often were redwood timbers laid directly on the ground, though sometimes bricks (usually dry stacked without mortar) were used. Framing and flooring were Douglas fir, siding was redwood (painted, usually white), and roofs were shingles of western red cedar. Some of the more lavish houses had oak floors, and interior paneling of varnished redwood. Mortared brick was used for chimneys, but not walls; it was too expensive and hard to come by. By the 1980's, increasing price of wood, and the objections of insurance companies to flammable construction, supported a shift toward concrete, metal, and stucco as common building materials. I know of only one house in the district built of native materials: it was a small farm-worker's shack built of crude adobe bricks from the local soil. When I went to photograph it in the spring of 2000, I found that it had been demolished. There is also one brick house in the district, dating from the 1920's.

The absence of stone, even in public buildings of the towns, probably does not reflect any disdain for stone, but only its unavailability in the district. Stone as a building material powerfully symbolizes the durability of the institution housed in the building, whether it is a bank or a government or a family. Stone buildings are built to last. This is usually reckoned to be a virtue, though I'm not so sure. Many old buildings are dark and uncomfortable and poorly thought out; better that they had been built of something less eternal than stone, so that they might gracefully perish when they had outlived their time.

We may think of a house as an object, but it might better be considered a process. In thermodynamic terms, a house is a nexus of matter and energy at a point far from equilibrium, and the forces of nature are persistent in their will to move it back to equilibrium. The tug of gravity, the steady ping of photons on the exposed surfaces, the prying of oxygen and ozone, the erosive flow of water and dust, the shoving of the wind, conspire to return the house to a heap of dust. The owner prevents this only by the continuous infusion of energy, or as he sees it, money, to stave off the forces of decay. But sometimes the owner lacks the resources, or the will, or the notion, to maintain his house, and it deteriorates.

The alert traveler in the countryside will find houses, or more often neighborhoods, passing through cycles of abandonment. Consider an example: A couple in their forties buy a two acre parcel and build a modest house, around which they construct a little farm. They have fruit trees and a vineyard, gardens, a greenhouse, a pond, poultry, a cow, a goat, and a few sheep, and they industriously maintain their little paradise. But they get old, and the place is too much for them, and the novelty has gone out of it, and it gradually runs down. The old fellow dies, and after a few years his widow moves to town, and the place is abandoned. Next the place is bought by a family with a daughter who is obsessed with horses. They spruce up the house, rip out the old sheds and gardens, and build a horse barn. A gleaming white fence in the Kentucky horse-estate style is set up on the perimeter, and the grounds put into pasture. But after a few years the daughter goes off to college, and discovers boys to be more interesting than horses, and seldom comes home. The horse is sold off, the paint peels on the fence, the pasture runs to thistle. With the horse gone, there is no reason to stay in the country, and the family moves back to town and leaves the place empty. A childless older couple, enthusiastic gardeners buy the place. They lay out paths and beds and lawns, erect pergolas and arbors and a fountain, and plant twenty-five-hundred different kinds of plants. But after a some years he throws a disk in his back, and she is disabled by arthritis in her hands, and the garden is left to fend for itself. The house roof leaks and is not fixed, a screen door hangs askew on rusted hinges, a broken window pane is patched with cardboard. Finally they move to a retirement home, and the place again is abandoned.

Cycles of abandonment such as that just described are a natural feature of the rural landscape. They

Figure 46. Abandoned farmstead. Yolo County

reflect the natural cycle of a human life: the infidelity of one's enthusiasms, and the gradual failure of one's strength even when the will is unwavering. But one does not see here the wholesale abandonment of farms, such as one has seen in the east since the eighteenth century when New England farmers abandoned their stony ground to move to fertile lands of Ohio. Farmland here has always been too valuable and too productive to be abandoned. What one does see is the abandonment of houses and barns and farmsteads. The family moves to town, and what had been the old home place is leased out to farm workers, who have few housekeeping skills, and no incentive to maintain the place. The next stage is abandonment. Goats inhabit the parlor, and possums nest in the stuffing of a decaying sofa.

It would be an error to think that the old mansions that still survive typify the nineteenth century housing of the district. They have survived because they were well built of good materials, and because they were too valuable to be allowed to perish. But the majority of houses were much humbler in scale and in materials, and most of them are gone. So we see now a landscape from which the commonest elements have been removed, and the exceptional ones remain. Each mansion was the center of a community of workers, who lived nearby in simple dwellings, or shacks, or tents. Travel on foot or horseback was slow; commuting was not an option, and the workers had to live on the farm.

Figure 47. Abandoned farmstead. The windmill tower remains (windmill gone); the tank remains, though the upper part of the tower is gone. The buildings are abandoned, but not the land, which is planted to a young almond orchard. Solano County

I once dismantled a hundred-twenty year old farm worker's house that was to be demolished. It was a simple building of a few hundred square feet, framed in fir, on a redwood foundation sitting directly on the ground, with rough redwood one by twelve boards nailed up vertically for siding, and no interior finish to the walls. There were two rooms, one with a wood-burning iron stove provided with a clay flue. The north wall of the north room had been papered with Chinese newspapers printed in Stockton, California, in 1886. The building had originally been occupied by a Chinese tenant farmer who grew fresh market produce on ten acres of leased land. More recently it had been occupied by Mexican workers, one of whom had penciled a calendar on the wall to track his hours of work:

L	M	M	J	V	S	D
		13	12	14	13½	7½
15	12½	14	14	12	13	8
13½	11	15				

Sunday was the day of rest, on which he worked only eight hours. An immense cottonwood tree shaded the structure, and framed an outdoor living space (where, presumably, a privy also once stood). Simple dwellings of this type were once common throughout the district, either isolated, or clustered near the big manor houses, but hardly any remain.

A variation of these shacks, more typical of the twentieth century than the nineteenth, was the labor camp, used to house seasonal migrant workers who came to pick orchard fruit or tomatoes. Early on the laborers were Chinese or Filipinos; later many were Japanese, and after 1945, most were Mexican. White workers were hardly known, except for middle-class stay-at-homes pressed into service during wartime. Some of the labor camps had large dormitory buildings plus a bath house and a mess hall; others were collections of shanties. Also common were seasonal labor camps made up of canvas tents, similar to a military encampment; rows of smaller tents housed half a dozen men each, and a huge tent served as a mess hall. These were still common into the 1950's; I remember envying the workers, who had what seemed to be such a festive place to live, reminiscent of a circus. The dwelling that I admired even more was a group of old railroad boxcars parked on a siding. They were painted yellow, and had windows cut into them; under the windows were window boxes with geraniums. As I child I could imagine no finer place to live.

The disappearance of humble housing in the district reflects changes in farming. Tomatoes, walnuts, prunes, and almonds are now harvested by machine, and large crews are no longer need to hand pick the fruit. Moreover, the low cost of used automobiles allows even the lowliest-paid worker to have a car, and so be able to live where he chooses—often in town.

The fine old nineteenth-century manor houses that persist in the district are not easily interpreted as landscape elements. At the time they were built they must have had a well-understood social significance, but the decades have ticked by and the houses are now bereft of context. What did their contemporaries make of the elaborate encrustation with architectural ornament? Was it seen as refined, or beautiful, or ostentatious, or more sympathetically, as architectural exuberance, celebrating the new technology of automatic power wood-shaping machinery that developed in the mid nineteenth century? We do not know. But human nature does not change so much in a century or two, and it seems likely that part of the symbolic role of the big house was a public display of prosperity and success of the farmer.

These old houses also reflect something of the social structure of the time, which was more hierarchical than present society. The traveler approaching a rural nineteenth century mansion in the district passed through a series of increasing intimacies (or for a stranger, increasing trespasses): from the public road to the private drive, to the front yard, perhaps passing through a gate in a low fence, to the steps, then ascending to the porch, across the porch, over the threshold past the massive front door with its impressive hardware, into a foyer, to the public rooms (living room, dining room), to the private rooms. Because the house was usually built on high ground, the approach entailed a slight ascent at each stage. This layout was designed as the physical counterpart of a social transition from public to private, dirty to clean, coarse to smooth, hot to cool (summer), cold to warm (winter), windy to still, and from the masculine world to the feminine world. The many stages of this transition permitted fine social distinctions. One guest might be admitted to the porch but not across the threshold; another less privileged might state his business from the base of the porch stairs, not feeling entitled to ascend.

An important social function of the private house is that it provides the opportunity to offer hospitality, one aspect of which is the conspicuous abandonment of defenses. The purpose of the brass bolts of the massive front door was not to keep uninvited people out—one could easily enough gain entry by a flimsy side door or back door—but to allow for their symbolic breaching as a mark of hospitality. Even though the family might come and go by the back door, it was important for guests to be admitted by the front door so that they would participate in the voluntary lowering of defenses. In the last fifty years, builders in the district have lost sight of this. Houses have confusing entrances; the 'front' door is off the side and never used, and the family comes and goes through the garage. The building fails to express the social relation, and the guest is confused about where to go and what is signified.

Whatever one might think of the aesthetics of modern rural houses in the district (and there are a handful of excellent ones among the general run of mediocrity), there is nonetheless a positive social message to be read. Compared to the scene of a hundred years ago, the modern landscape is far more egalitarian. Where once there were manor houses and shanties, and some in-between houses as well, there is now a relative uniformity in the social stature of rural houses. The most lavish does not differ greatly in materials or style or size from the humblest. Everyone has heat. Everyone has indoor plumbing. Everyone has electricity and a telephone and a refrigerator. Equality in housing reflects equality in society. We have made some progress here.

BARNS

Unlike houses, for which no vernacular architectural tradition developed, barns have a characteristic construction throughout the region. Their uniformity is not surprising, since most were built by just a few contractors who specialized in barns. For the farmer who would build his own barn, kits were locally available, having been shipped around Cape Horn or sent cross country by railroad from New York or Philadelphia. The kit included architectural plans and elevations for the barn, plus the metal hardware: hinges, latches, rolling door track, hay trolley and track, cast-iron rafter ties, and kegs of nails.

There are two principal variants of nineteenth-century barns in the district. One is a rectangular structure with two gabled ends and a steeply pitched roof (usually ten in twelve). Within, four rows of posts define three bays running the length of the barn, the central bay with rolling doors at one or both ends. The bays are of equal width, fourteen feet being typical, making a forty-two foot wide barn, though barns forty-eight and fifty-four feet wide can be found in the

Figure 48. Classic barn. Yolo County

district. A length of seventy-two to ninety-six feet was common. In the second variant, only one end is gabled , and the other is a hipped gable. The hipped end has triangular shapes that greatly strengthen the entire structure.

The oaks, cottonwoods, and walnuts of the district have twisty, branching trunks, unsuited to hewing out a long straight beam, so that timber-framed barns typical of the eastern US were not practical. However, sawed lumber was readily available from forests east and west of the valley: cedar for roof shingles from the Sierra Nevada, redwood for the foundations and exterior siding from the coast range, and Douglas fir from either range. (In the course of dismantling old barns I have noticed that Port Orford cedar was commonly mixed in with Douglas fir for the 1x6 skip sheathing on the roof, suggesting a north coast provenance.) The efficient manufacture of nails had been worked out in the first half of the nineteenth century, with their price dropping by ninety percent, so the price of a keg of nails was not prohibitive, and a barn held together with nails rather than pegs was feasible. The biggest timbers in the building—the central two rows of posts—were only 4x6's, though as much as thirty feet long, and often straight-grained and knot free at that.

Frequently, the farmer would find himself needing more barn space after a few years, and so the barn would be expanded by adding sheds to the two long sides and to one gable end, hipped where they met at the corner. Because the height of the side walls of the original barn was already low, the steep pitch of the original roof could not be maintained in the addition, and so a shallower pitch (four in twelve) was used. The result is a strikingly beautiful roof line; the roof seems the epitome of shelter, like a great bird with wings spread, protecting its young.

In use, the central bay of a livestock barns was for traffic, and the side bays were used for storing equipment and for housing mules and horses and dairy cows. The central bay had a floor ten or twelve feet up, creating a loft in which hay was stored. Hay was brought in from the fields piled loose on a wagon, and placed in the loft using a trolley that ran along a track fastened to the underside of the ridge beam. This track extended five or six feet beyond the gable end so that hay could be lifted vertically from the wagon to the ridge, using pulleys and draft animals for lifting power, before being moved into the loft. The extension of the hay trolley track accounts for the 'beak' on one or both gable ends of an old barn. With hay in the loft, the farmer could feed his stock with gravity in his favor, by pitching the hay downward through a system of hatches and

Figure 49. Modern steel hay barn, covering an acre and a half of ground. Yolo County

chutes. Some barns were used only for hay. They had a track and trolley, but no loft, and an enormous haystack was built inside the barn, nearly filling it. I know of one old hay barn in Yolo County that was converted for grain storage. A concrete floor was poured, with iron rings in the floor anchoring chains that attached to the top plate of the side walls. The chains kept the walls from bursting outward from the pressure of the grain within.

Orientation of the barn was square to the road, but beyond that there seems no preference. In the prairie states, barns uniformly turn their backs to the north, where nasty weather comes from. In this district we have winds from the north, but winter storms from the south, and so there is no obvious best orientation, and barns can be found with their doors facing any of the cardinal directions.

The last of the classic regional barns was built before the great depression. After that, the old style of barn no longer suited the needs of farmers. The mules and horses were replaced by machines, some so big that they could not fit through the old barn doors. The baling and handling of hay also became fully mechanized. Barns built from the 1930's to the 1970's represent a miscellany of styles. New materials—plywood and corrugated steel—came into use, and the steep pitch of a roof that accommodated a hay loft gave way to low roofs. Many barns of this era are not particularly handsome, but there are some notable exceptions (for example, figure 51). By the 1970s, steel clad barns with a steel frame became the norm. Some of these are tremendous, covering more than an acre. To my eye these structures have neither grace nor charm. In their similarity to industrial buildings, the newer barns seem to propagate a false metaphor, that farming is an industry, and the field a factory.

There were once a dozen to fifteen old barns to the square mile in the district. Every year or two

Figure 50. Abandoned barn. Yolo County

Figure 51. An architecturally harmonious collection of barns, circa 1952. Solano County

now another of the old barns is torn down. I have myself dismantled a few that were slated for demolition, in order to salvage the lumber. The dark interior of an old barn, long shafts of light slanting from a missing roof shingle, pigeons cooing in the loft, has always seemed to me a more numinous space than any church. When I was a child, the hay loft of such a barn was my destination on a rainy Saturday, when I might lay in the fragrant hay, and listen to the rain, and the scratching of mice. It is sad to see them go. Even if a few were protected as historic structures, it is not the same as the preservation of an extended landscape dotted with such barns, any more than the preservation of a few endangered bison in a zoo substitutes for preservation of the great wild herds.

TANK TOWERS

In hilly country the domestic water supply can be located uphill from the house with the elevation providing water pressure. But in the flat country around central Putah Creek, water has to be elevated in a man-made structure. Usually this was a tank tower (though a farm in Yolo County where I lived in the 1950's had a water tank high in the barn). The logic of the tank tower is that a windmill pumps water only when the wind is blowing, and even then the flow is irregular. By storing water in an elevated tank, water would be always available, and at even pressure. The earliest tanks were redwood, but by 1900 steel tanks were common. Two thousand gallons was a typical size. Water gains pressure at about two thirds of a pound per foot of elevation, so that to have reasonable water pressure in the house (20-30 pounds per square inch) requires the tank to be thirty to forty feet above the ground. The result is a tall, skinny building with eight tons of water at the top—an unfortunate construct in a countryside subject to earthquakes.

To strengthen the tower, and to increase its stability, the walls below the tank were flared outward. The resulting structure, with its tapered walls and pyramidal roof, is the most characteristic architectural feature of the district. Although most of the tank towers in the district were built by one contractor (Johnson Tank and Tower of Fairfield), it seems that no two are exactly alike. Many variations in siding materials and in the design and placement of vents, windows, and applied ornaments gives each its character.

Often a windmill was attached to one side or a corner of the tank tower. Occasionally a tank tower may be found with three tapered corners and one straight corner. Study the ground and you will likely discover the remains of a well at the base of the vertical corner. On the Hamel Ranch in Solano County there is a tank tower, directly adjacent to Interstate 80 so that it is well known, that has a windmill mounted on the peak of the roof. This is not a functional windmill. It was put there as a visual joke. When it was operating the windmill was mounted to one side of the tower.

With the spread of rural electrification and the advent of electric pumps and steel pressure tanks, tank towers were no longer needed, and by the 1930's they were no longer being built. I know of none that is in use today for its original purpose. A few have been converted to other uses, but it takes uncommon imagination to make use of a building that is sixteen feet square and forty feet tall. About seventy tank towers remain in the district.

The principle of the tank tower—elevating water to provide steady pressure unaffected by power failures—is still used in town. Massive steel water towers, the only sign of town visible from ten miles away, are the unlikely modern descendents of the old rural tank towers.

WINDMILLS

One of the most conspicuous elements of the rural built environment was the water-pumping windmill. Typically the wind-

Figure 52. Tank tower ca. 1890 with remains of an IXL open gear windmill. Solano County

Figure 54. Classic tank tower. The beam projecting from the left wall stabilized the windmill. Solano County

Figure 53. Tank tower ca. 1910 with its original open gear windmill still intact. Furiously barking dogs discouraged a closer inspection. Solano County

Figure 55. Vertical siding on a tank tower is rarely seen. Yolo County

mill was set on a tower thirty to forty feet tall, to place the mill at an altitude where the breezes are stronger and more consistent. Alternatively, it was mounted to one corner, or side, of a tank tower. The mill is mounted on a bearing that allows it to turn into the wind, filling the function of a weather vane. There is an old windmill on my place, and I frequently consult it to know what the wind is doing at thirty-five feet up.

Many think of the windmill as a nineteenth century contraption, but most of them are more modern than that. The windmills of the early settlers were noisy, inefficient, and unreliable devices with wooden wheels and open gears. The all-steel windmills became common only in the 1880's. The early ones had open gears that were supposed to be greased once a week, (but probably seldom were). The first modern windmill, with gears running in an oil-filled crankcase, requiring only an annual oil change, was the Elgin Wonder Model B, which debuted in 1912. Windmill production reached its peak in the second decade of the twentieth century, and remained strong until World War II.

I know of remains of about 30 windmills in the district, but only two of them still pump water. There is a surprising diversity of manufacturers: Aermotor, Baker, Dempster, Stover, Flint and Walling, Fairbanks-Morse, IXL, and Elgin. In contrast, all of the windmills that I have seen around Rio Vista, thirty miles to the south, where they are common, are Aermotor 702's.

The ability of a windmill to pump water depends on speed of the wind, height that the water is to be lifted, and diameter of the wheel. A ten-foot diameter mill on a breezy day can pump 2-300 gallons of water per hour from a depth of fifty feet. On a still day it pumps nothing at all. This output is sufficient to run a household and water the livestock and irrigate a kitchen garden. But it does not begin to suffice for irrigation of crops (despite the name of one popular brand— 'The Irrigator'). So the windmills supplied houses and stock-watering stations only; irrigation of

Figure 56. Flint & Walling Star 24 windmill with steel tower. Solano County

crops came in later with the use of petroleum-powered motors.

In operation, a windmill combines motion, noise, and flowing water in a confabulation of clanking, squeaking, and splashing—irresistible to boys of all ages. But in addition to its mechanical fascination, the windmill is a symbol of water in a seasonal desert, one of the essential components of a homestead and a prerequisite for settlement.

Some of the windmills in the district date from the 1920's and 30's, long after rural electrification. It is a puzzle to know why a farmer would choose a windmill over a more reliable and less expensive electric pump. Perhaps the farmer was not in a hurry to put himself at the mercy of a monopoly (the power company) after his bad experience with another monopoly (the railroad).

FENCES

In the century following California statehood, hundreds of miles of fences were built in the Putah Creek region. Much hard human labor went into these fences—digging holes in unyielding ground, tamping the soil around the posts, stretching heavy wire. The redwood posts were riven rather than sawn, split by hand with wedges and mauls from redwood stumps. Century-old posts are still common in the region. Charred by grass-fires, punctuated by fence staples long since rusted away, they have a rugged individuality to them. Mounted on a white wall in an art gallery, they would be admired as artifacts of great character. But in place in the field, they are not much noticed. The horizontal elements of the earliest fences were redwood planks, but by the 1880's woven or knotted wire fencing became common, stapled to the posts, usually topped with a strand or two of barbed wire. These fences are easily hopped over, and do not much trouble the foot traveler.

The old fences were meant to confine livestock, and keep it from

Figure 57. Star 24 windmill with a homemade wooden tower. Yolo County

wandering. They were enclosures, fencing-in fences. The fencerows created a habitat in which native plants could persist undisturbed by plowing, and provided a home to rabbits and snakes and other small animals. But with the waning of livestock culture, and the replacement of draft animals by tractors, the fences were no longer needed and many have been pulled out. The fenceless ground is more easily farmed. There is no impediment to the free movement of tractors, and no source of weeds at the field's perimeter, which usually is graded smooth.

As the old fences are in decline, a new kind of fence is showing up in the region. This is a fence of exclusion rather than of enclosure—a fencing-out fence. Stoutly and expensively built of steel, these fences are marked every few hundred feet by a 'No Trespassing' sign. The fencing-out fences typically surround lands owned by corporations, or absentee owners, or urban immigrants. They express distrust and hostility. They say to the foot-traveler: 'I am wealthy. I have nasty lawyers. I do not share. Keep out!. A heavy application of herbicides along the fence keeps the ground barren, and gives a prison-perimeter look.

Figure 58. Fairbanks-Morse open gear windmill, ca. 1880. Only the gears remain. Solano County

Another kind of fence common in the district is neatly built of sawn boards, painted white. The white fences indicate that these are the lands of people who keep horses. They read glossy magazines picturing lush ranches in Kentucky and Florida where white fences surround a well-groomed turf, and they emulate this image, which has more reality to them than the muted and arid landscape before their eyes. The whiteness of the fence, so impractical and so unnatural, calls attention to itself. It is both a fencing-in fence and a fencing-out fence, but more than either of those it is a symbolic fence, expressing the allegiance of the owners to the values of the wealthy and conservative class of people who keep thoroughbred horses. It is a badge of membership in an exclusive club. To one who is not a member of that club, the fence has more ominous connotations. This is a fence far from equilibrium, one that can be maintained only with considerable energy: regular hoeing out of the weeds, and an annual whitewashing. One does not imagine that

Figure 59. Horse fences. Yolo County

the owner of the Kentucky estate is out there painting the fence himself; implicit in the fence is the notion that there are slaves, or their modern equivalents, to maintain it.

A neighbor of mine kept a horse. He didn't have a white horse fence; just a mongrel sort of fence confabulated of old railroad ties and cast-off scantlings. One morning I was out before dawn setting irrigation, and I noticed my neighbor's horse, which had escaped. He was standing in my garden, eating okra. I went inside and telephoned my neighbor. 'Your horse is loose,' I said. 'He's over here.' Twenty minutes later I could see my neighbor and his wife in a safflower field. They were waving and hollering at the horse, who was trotting southward through open country. He stopped for a moment and looked back over his shoulder at them, his eyes shining with contempt.

ORDER AND DISORDER

The architecture of rural buildings and their arrangement on the land is only part of their character. The habits of the owners or tenants also color the picture. Perhaps the most evident character trait is the tendency toward orderliness, or its opposite.

Some farmsteads are a chronic mess. The driveway is riddled with ruts and pits, and in the rainy season the tenants take novel routes across the yard or through bushes to avoid getting stuck. A pile of pallets, moldering with age, that were intended for making into a picket fence, are heaped to one side of the yard. Plastic children's toys are strewn about, and a bored Labrador roped to a veranda post chews on the shredded wheel of a tricycle. Someone started to paint the house in a dramatic combination of maroon and silver, but the job was abandoned months ago, and the ladder still leans against a half-painted wall. A pickup truck is parked under a tree; its motor, which dangles from a chain hoist looped over a branch, turns slowly in the wind. Some salvaged rolls of wire fencing, tossed off a truck and forgotten, have become cylindrical topiaries of bindweed. A pair of Muscovy ducks wanders the yard, squatting here and there to leave little decorations. A heap of black plastic bags of garbage were meant to be taken to the dump, but raccoons have got into them, and now a long stream of trash demonstrates the direction of the prevailing wind. Next to a tumbled-down chicken coop, a '66 Volvo with a cracked windshield sits on four flat tires; a goat stands on its roof, gazing at the world with amber eyes.

What can be going on in the minds of the people who live here? I think it must be a combination of mental blindness and an excess of imagination. For the most part, they simply do not see the chaos in which they live. Their attention is elsewhere. And when, for some reason, they do notice something, they imagine what it should have been instead of seeing what it is. Should they happen to take notice of the pile of pallets, they immediately see in their imagination the white picket fence that the pallets were supposed to have become. And the old Volvo with the goat on the roof they see in their mind's eye as an immaculately restored classic, motoring smoothly down the road while awed bystanders look on in admiration. It is a triumph of dreaming over reality.

Luckily, the highly disordered farmsteads are rare. Most places are middling. A little bit of shabbiness starts to creep in, and then the place gets cleaned up. Perhaps guests are coming to dinner and so the rose prunings get taken to the burn pile and the lawn is mowed and the boxes of bottles and newspapers are taken to the recycling center. Then things gradually slide toward disorder again until a few weeks later there is another episode of cleaning up.

At the other end of the spectrum are places that suggest a pathological degree of orderliness. The lawn is mowed twice a week, and fallen leaves are raked from it within an hour of falling. The bushes are severely pruned; the trunks of trees might be painted white. The windows of the house are washed fortnightly, inside and out, and the Buick in the garage, a Bush-Cheney sticker on its bumper, is dusted daily. In the equipment shed, the correct positions of machines is marked on the concrete floor so that they can be parked in perfect alignment. The owner's blue jeans are ironed, with a crease. His orchard is laid out with a laser so that the lines of trees can be perfectly straight.

In a way, extreme orderliness is a more disturbing sight than disorderliness. It expresses a discomfort with nature, which, after all, is rather shaggy around the edges. And the excessively orderly farmer is likely to have too heavy a hand with herbicides, and to have too low of a threshold for spraying insecticides. He probably mows and cultivates more often than is needed. At the extreme, orderliness becomes a form of intolerance.

Figure 60. Modern tract housing with large houses, small lots. Yolo County

Chapter Ten:

Town

HOUSING

Housing occupies most of the area of the town, and new housing is the most voracious consumer of open land in the district. The nature of single family housing has evolved in a very consistent way over the last century, and in order to understand housing, or houses, as a landscape element, we have to investigate some of the forces driving the housing market.

In 1900, a typical single family dwelling had two bedrooms and one bath, and an area of 600 square feet. Often the house had no closets, for there was nothing to put in a closet. Material culture was simple, and much of daily life was passed on the front porch, where one might enjoy the evening breeze, and visit with neighbors passing by on foot. By 1950, three bedrooms and a thousand square feet were the norm. By 1970, three bedrooms, two baths, and 1500 square feet typified new housing. In the year 2000, a new house has four or five bedrooms, three baths, a three-car garage, and 3000 square feet of living space. And, contrary to the growing size of houses, families are smaller than they were a century ago.

In part, people need bigger houses because they have more stuff. During the twentieth century the manufacture and distribution of goods became enormously efficient. The price of virtually all goods, measured in constant terms, declined, and an increment of labor now buys far more than it did. Not only that, but many new kinds of goods have been invented: computers, televisions, microwave ovens, scuba gear, jet skis, and much other such stuff that was unheard of a generation ago is now reckoned a necessity. An optimist might say that we have mastered the material world; a more sanguine critic might say that it has mastered us.

It is also true that daily life has increasingly moved indoors. The aboriginal inhabitants of the district lived outside, and entered their huts only to sleep or to sit out stormy weather. But now people, even children, are seldom out of doors. Indoor life has been made more attractive and comfortable with heat and air conditioning, good lighting, refrigeration, television, and recorded music, and this might justify a need for more interior space. In addition, the outside world has steadily been degraded. Where one might once have sat on the porch of a summer's evening, listening to the rustling of the leaves in the delta breeze, one now is oppressed by booming music from passing cars, the roar of engines, the sound of sirens. The gentle skritch of a bamboo rake has been replaced by the insane scream of a leaf blower. Outdoors is not what it used to be. People take refuge in their homes.

But more than either of these, the chief determinant of the size of houses is the price of land. When land is expensive, builders put up big houses. If a bare lot costs one hundred thousand dollars, and if building a house costs one hundred dollars per square foot, then one could build a 600 square foot house for $160,000 ($100,000 for the lot, plus $60,000 for the house). Doubling the size of the house to 1200 square feet makes a cost of $220,000 ($100,000 for the lot, plus $120,000) for the house. The result is that one can get twice as much house (1200 instead of 600 square feet) for only a 37% increase in the total price. This is an irresistible economic force. Empirically, the total cost—house plus lot—will not drop below two and a half times the cost of the lot. So if lots sell for $125,000, which is a typical low end price today, the finished house will be not less than $312,000. And the house one gets for $312,000 will be big and fancy, not small and humble.

This situation has profound implications in many areas, including the subject of this book (landscape) and also the social structure of the town. Expensive, detached, single-family dwellings are bought by expensive, detached, single families. The father's an attorney, the mother's a doctor, and they have 1.5 children and 3.2 automobiles. In 1910 an average house cost about one year's salary of an average worker. By 2000, an average new house in Davis costs about seven years' salary of an average worker. The self-employed artist, the farm-worker with five children, the single mother, are squeezed out of the picture.

The styles of architecture of houses in town do not differ from the styles of houses in the countryside built at the same time. One can imagine the townscape as simply a compressed rural landscape. The town house was a farm house placed on an eighth of an acre instead of on 160 acres. Architecturally, the town house makes no acknowledgement of its neighbors; it occupies its plot as if surrounded by fields. Windows are placed on all sides without regard to a neighbor's window a few feet away. This is not a problem when the houses are small compared to the size of the lots. But in the modern tracts the lots are smaller and smaller and the houses bigger and bigger until each house is staring furiously, eyeball to eyeball, at its neighbor, only a few feet away. Big houses, so close together, seem confrontational. And yet, the developers are unwilling to take the obvious next step of a shared common wall and a row of town houses. And the smaller the yard, the sturdier and taller the fence, for it is the smallest territories that are most fiercely held.

In Spain, or Morocco, this problem is solved by using a fundamentally different notion of a house. Instead of outward looking, it is introspective; it turns its back to its neighbors and looks into its own interior courtyard. The courtyard, with its trickling fountain, potted lemon trees, drying laundry, a bicycle leaning against a wall, is an attractive space, out of doors, and yet private and protected from the chaos of the streets. This style of housing would be entirely appropriate in this region, perhaps more so than what we have, but real estate developers and the bankers who back them are notorious for their conservatism and lack of imagination, and so Mediterranean urban housing has never been attempted here. It is also true that the free-stranding house is a direct descendent of the pioneer homestead. However much the tract house might differ from a pioneer cabin, it is nonetheless a remnant of a deeply ingrained rural tradition and an important symbol.

In some neighborhoods, lots have been sold to independent owners or builders, and the houses put up one by one. This is not always a success. What is one to make of a pseudo-Virginia colonial adjacent to a Spanish hacienda adjacent to a Cape Cod saltbox adjacent to an Arizona ranch, complete with trucked in boulders and bleached cow skull? The spectator is expected to suspend his disbelief, and to imagine each house as if it were solitary, with an appropriate landscape extending to the horizon. This type of neighborhood expresses a denial of urbanity, and harkens to the myth of the pioneer with his isolated rural homestead. Sometimes tract housing, however raw and discouraging when new, has a more harmonious outcome than an excess of individualism.

Much of the tract housing build in the 1950's and 1960's was poor in design and execution, but the houses were small and on large lots, and the owners have wrought their dreams on them, adding and remodeling until the casual observer will fail to notice that the houses were once all the same. With the newer tract housing, the big houses are built fully to the legal setbacks on their small lots. Future additions to the houses will not be possible, and the character of the neighborhood will evolve only by the growth of trees and development of gardens. What had formerly been house-as-process has become house-as-object.

The quality of housing in town is, on the average, mediocre. Which is not to say that people do not lead happy and fulfilled lives in these houses. But rather that the same materials and same labor could have been used to make a far better house, if only more thought and care had gone into it. Mixed in with the general run are a number of excellent houses: some excellent and modest (a combination of traits as becoming to a house as to a person), others excellent and flamboyant. There is a small part of the populace, just a few percent, who passionately care about their house as a work of art, and these few should have the opportunity to build their houses as they envision them. But for the majority of people, tract housing, if it is well executed, is very adequate. And the quality of tract housing being built at present is much improved over what was being built thirty years ago.

The styles of houses are very much subject to fashion, and it is no more difficult to date a twentieth century house to its proper decade than to date an automobile. This is evident in many details; as just one example, consider windows. Early in the century wood double-hung windows were the norm, usually with just the upper sash divided into six panes. By the 1920's, steel casement windows divided into rectangular panes also came into fashion. In the thirties and forties, advances in the technology of glass making made large pieces of plate glass available inexpensively, and 'picture windows' became common. The advertising of that era is ambiguous about what is meant by the 'picture.' Is it the view that the inhabitant of the house sees, usually a garden with birds at a feeder and a distant clump of trees, when he looks out the picture window? Or is it the domestic tableau that a passerby might see as he looks into the house, the inhabitants unashamedly (and with a trace of exhibitionism) presenting their blameless lives to the scrutiny of a voyeur? No nasty little habits to be hidden here. By the 1950's the trend was for windows framed in aluminum—a modern material hinting of technological advances in aeronautics. In the 1970's the mill-finish aluminum was replaced by black or bronze. In the 1980's grids of faux muntins were added. Ten years later white was the fashionable color of window frames—black ones could be secured only by special order.

DYNAMICS OF URBAN GROWTH

New housing is built at the periphery of the town, since there is no available space in the middle. And because the size of houses has increased steadily over the last century, we find the smallest houses in the center of town, with progressively large (newer) houses as one moves toward the perimeter. But the rising price of land at the perimeter does not affect just the perimeter—it also affects the center of town; a rising tide floats all boats. If a sixty-foot lot on the edge of town is worth $125,000, then a similar lot in the center of town is worth at least that, and perhaps more. As a consequence, the value of houses in the center of town becomes out of balance with the value of the land on which they sit. At present there is a 400 square foot house for sale in the center of town at $200,000. Clearly it is expected that the buyer would demolish the house and put up a far more valuable building that is in balance with the value of the land.

So if new construction at the periphery of town is one half of urban growth, the other half is the demolition of buildings in the center and

Figure 61. Tree-shaded streets in an old part of town. Yolo County

their replacement by buildings of greater value. This mechanism of growth has been well known for many years. Study the history of any city—Sacramento, San Francisco, New York, Boston—and you will find perfectly good buildings being torn down because they can no longer justify the value of the land on which they sit.

One other aspect of the dynamics of urban growth deserves mention, and it has to do not with houses but with trees. New development takes place on former agricultural fields, which are treeless. And so in the new tracts the houses and pavement dominate the scene; the few saplings are hardly notable in the landscape. But as the neighborhood matures, the trees overshadow the houses and become the dominant feature of the landscape. A shady street on a hot summer day is the most attractive and inviting aspect of an old neighborhood, especially compared to baking expanse of stucco and asphalt in the new tracts.

The process in the center of town, of replacing older buildings with newer ones as a consequence of rising land values, runs into a problem on the issue of historic preservation. There are old structures whose historic, symbolic, or aesthetic value exceeds their value as simply so many square feet of enclosed space, and often such buildings deserve preservation. It is best when intact historic neighborhoods can be preserved, but usually the worthy buildings are not clumped together but are scattered here and there. A historic small house flanked by three-story commercial blocks is badly out of context. The historic buildings in Davis are almost all light frame structures which are easily moved, and there would be some logic into clustering them together in a historic zone. There is already a history of this, for example, moving the old library from F street to Central Park, or moving Wyatt Pavilion across the north fork of Putah Creek.

THE EDGE OF TOWN

The attentive world traveler will have noticed that the most appealing landscapes are to be found where there is a clear distinction between town and country. The hill towns of Tuscany, farming villages of rural Japan, and hamlets of northern Scotland are examples. You reach the edge of town, and then you are in the country; there is no ambiguity. The alternative is an ill-defined boundary with fragments of urbanization strung out along the roads leading from town, so that the traveler is hard pressed to say when it is that he has truly arrived in town, or left town.

The two towns in the district—Winters and Davis—each have some boundaries that are well-defined and others that are blurred. In both, the indistinct boundary occurs in relationship to an interstate highway: I-505 passing east of Winters and I-80 angling through the southeast quadrant of Davis. The freeway is incompatible with urban values, and throws the boundary into disarray. Wherever it goes, the freeway is a barrier in much the same way that a major river is a barrier. But at the edge of a town it is also a source of visual confusion. Traffic on the city streets moves slowly, while it moves three times as fast on the adjacent freeway, so that we have to devote an unreasonable amount of our attention to reconciling the disparate speeds of moving vehicles in our field of view. And where the freeway skirts a town, signs are erected, and because traffic is fast, the signs have to be big to be seen. And so we have a landscape filled with large words, which is visually discomforting.

Figure 62. Tract housing is a voracious consumer of farm land. Yolo County

The symbolism of the written word is too powerful to be ignored. A word writ large in the landscape is like someone shouting at you, and when the written words are many, the result is a cacophony of shouting, mostly of messages that you do not wish to hear. I have noticed that when I have traveled abroad in lands where I do not understand the alphabet (China, Thailand) the signs are not at all bothersome, but are merely interesting ornaments and decorations. The same signage in English would be distressing. Part of the charm of the rural countryside is the absence of the written word in the landscape.

In both Davis and Winters urban growth is controversial, but there seems always to be agreement that an increase in population also requires moving the edge of town further out into the countryside and increasing the area of the town. Indeed, real estate developers who hold title to lands on the periphery of town are impatient for the chance to finally grab their millions. But the linkage of population growth with expansion of the city limits is a false notion, and should be rejected. It comes from maintaining the rural tradition of housing that has evolved into tract housing, instead of embracing a truly urban approach to housing. The fortified medieval town had a perimeter defined by the city wall, and all growth took place within that boundary. Similarly, Davis or Winters could define its perimeter with a greenbelt, perhaps ornamented with jogging and cycling paths, and declare, 'This is it. This is the edge of town, for ever more.' Growth of the urban population would still be allowed, by increasing density, and by erection of taller buildings. The result would inescapably be superior to continuing suburban sprawl, no matter how much the populations of the towns grew. Growth restricted by area but not number of citizens would force a diversification of building styles that would better serve the needs of the citizens than what we have now. And such a limitation of growth would protect farmland that currently is vulnerable to urbanization.

OPEN SPACE

Open space in Davis is of two sorts: space devoted to the automobile (streets and parking lots), which is the majority, and parks, including the small private parks (gardens) surrounding each house, and the public parks and schoolyards. In the last half century the nature of public space (parks and schoolyards) has undergone a curious transformation.

Fifty years ago there was only one park in town, Central Park, a square block bordered by fourth, fifth, B and C streets. The park had a swing and a slide for children; other than that it was trees and grass. On the fourth of July the entire town (2,000 people) met at the park for a potluck dinner and fireworks; if your last name starts with A through E bring a salad, F through L bring a dessert, etc. The schools were the elementary school (demolished 1966) occupying the block south of Central Park, and the High School diagonally northwest of the park. The high school had playing fields consisting of a quarter-mile track with a football field marked off in the enclosed space, and a makeshift baseball diamond. Soccer, tennis, and golf were unknown.

Since then, the population of the town has increased thirty-fold, and the area of parks and schoolyards has increased proportionately, so that the square foot of parks per capita is about the same. But the nature of the parks has changed. Most of the space is meticulously laid out into playing fields. There are special fields for soccer, football, field hockey and baseball, as well as semi-public space devoted to golf. The baseball fields in particular are intensively developed with special materials on the ground, backdrops, fencing, netting, and massive banks of lights on eighty-foot poles. It is unthinkable that one might play soccer, or throw a Frisbee, on a baseball diamond, nor would one play baseball on a field used at other seasons for soccer. Each piece of ground has been committed to a very narrow use, often leaving it idle much of the year.

This notion of narrowly restricting the use of public space is part of the pseudo-professionalization of children's games. It used to be that play was spontaneous; some sort of field was laid out with a few shirts or school books marking the corners, rules were extemporized, and disputes were settled creatively by the children themselves. But adults have taken control of the games, which are now overlain with a heavy hand of authority. Fields are laid out by regulation to within a quarter inch in a hundred feet. The teams must have specific uniforms, and follow a schedule established months in advance. Arcane rules are enforced by adults with whistles and clipboards, and the wins and losses of the season are carefully reckoned. Children's games are now meant to be painstakingly detailed imitations of games played by adults on television.

Football is a corporate game; there is management (the backfield) and labor (the front line). Baseball, on the other hand, is a loose federation of independent players. Soc-

Figure 63. Public park designated for baseball: expensive to build, expensive to maintain, and hardly used. The high-intensity lighting is an economically and ecologically inappropriate use of electricity, and denies the natural rhythm of day and night. Yolo County

cer, field hockey, and basketball are true team sports, in which a sort of super-organism, the team, surpasses the sum of its individual parts. Despite these variations, all of these sports share a common social content: the rationale of the encounter is to determine a winner and a loser. The establishment and maintenance of dominance hierarchies is a genetic trait of many vertebrates, including humans. This trait need not be so nakedly expressed. There are cultures in which this instinct has been channeled into art, music, labor, personal creativity. But in our hypercompetitive society, in which even art and music and dance become the subject of competitions, the spontaneous play of children has been subverted into a formal system of confrontations to determine dominance.

If you watch the soccer games on a Saturday morning, you will notice quite a difference between the girls' games and the boys' games. For the boys, the game is surrogate warfare—establishing dominance is all that counts. But the girls seem more interested in the convivial tribalism of their team: the colorful uniforms, the totemic name (the 'Ladybugs,' the 'Blue Hummingbirds,' the 'Pink Dolphins'), the ritual chants. If it weren't for the screeching adults at the sidelines, they probably would pay little attention to who wins or loses.

Like the other games, golf requires commitment of a tract of land to a single narrow use. The golf course, with all the untidiness and unpredictability of the natural world removed, is like an illustration from a child's story book, or a Disney cartoon. Everything is neat and orderly—the trees, the greens, the paths, the perfectly edged ponds. And the golfer, too, with his brick red shirt and lemon yellow trousers and floppy green hat, seems to be a character from a story book. As a landscape, the golf course is an expurgated version of nature for those uncomfortable with the real natural world. Golf is perhaps the only one of the common sports that was not originally competitive. In its origins, golf was either an amusing adjunct to a solitary tramp through the sheep pastures, or an ornament to a congenial walk with friends. One's opponent, always, is one's self. It has no element of ritual warfare, though promoters of competitions have tried to twist it in that direction.

The conversion of public open space to arenas for surrogate warfare is unfortunate. Only a small portion of the population is able to use this space; much of it is idle and deserted through most of the year. Baseball is the worst offender, because of its unwillingness to share, its high capital costs, its high maintenance costs, and its perverse use of powerful lighting so that the game can be played at night. The failure of public space used for sports may be highlighted by comparing it to an unstructured public space—the original Central Park.

In the early 1990's Central Park doubled its size by taking over the abandoned schoolyard on the adjacent block to the south. A roof covering a twice weekly farmers market has been added, but the remaining ground is still unstructured—there are no playing fields laid out. It is widely agreed that Central Park, especially when the farmers market is in session, is the heart of the community. On a Wednesday evening in summer the park fills with people. The farmers are there with their piles of fruits and vegetables and buckets of flowers brought in from the countryside. Local chefs set up outdoor kitchens and display their skills in preparing dinner for the citizens. The local brewery offers beer on tap for the adults. A band plays. People take their dinners to the lawns, and sit and talk with their friends. Children and dogs frolic, or dance to the music.

Several features of this scene make it especially appealing. One is the absence of conflict that typifies parks laid out as playing fields.. No dominance is being expressed or challenged, there are no winners or losers, no ritual warfare is enacted. Even young feral males, usually the worst offenders, are on good behavior; some slink through the market, others strut in a cloud of unmerited self-esteem. And unlike the playing fields, this park does not have a few players and a mob of spectators; everyone here is a player. Another appealing feature of the park is that nothing is fake. The produce offered for sale is fresh, brought in directly from local fields by the farmers who grew it; the food is genuine, prepared on the spot; the music is live; the conversation is authentic and spontaneous, not something from a video screen. There is also a notable absence of machines. True, a row of dusty trucks belonging to the farmers is parked to one side, but the visitor can do his shopping, buy his dinner, visit with his friend, enjoy the music, and so pass the evening without operating any device, electronic or mechanical. This is how mammals are supposed to live. The popularity of the park demonstrates that this is the rightful use of public open space.

TURF

A lawn of turf grass occurs naturally in country that has a cool foggy climate and an abundance of grazing animals, such as sheep. It is no accident that both turf and golf are native to Scotland. In north America, turf was unknown until the twentieth century. In the eastern half of the country, a rough meadow, scythed a few times a year, served as a greensward around buildings. In the west, open ground around buildings was bare ground, perhaps with a few clumps of native bunch grasses that were dormant through the dry season. It was only with refinements in irrigation and the development of lawn mowing machines that the spread of turf beyond its natural habitats became common. In the second half of the twentieth century, turf lawns became universal, not only in the east, but in the west. The spread of lawns as a ubiquitous feature of the home grounds demonstrates the power of the magazines and television in successful promoting a notion that makes no ecological sense whatsoever. Turf survives in the west only with elaborate inputs of water, fertilizers, pesticides, fossil fuels, and human labor. In the district, the turf lawn is an unambiguous denial of the reality of where we live.

The townsman who buys a place in the country often puts in a full acre of lawn, imitating some notion of grandness from a television show. He buys a little riding lawnmower, and spends his weekend steering around the yard in a cloud of blue smoke, making an appalling racket, maiming the grasses, and imagining that he is doing something admirable.

BIG TOWN OR SMALL CITY?

Davis has reached a size where it is increasingly unrealistic to think of it as a town. It is time for the planners and city officials to shift their thinking from 'town' to 'small city'. A town does not suddenly become a city by reaching a certain population, however. There are cities in Greece and Italy of only a thousand people. What makes them cities is the culture, and the architecture, and the prizing of sociability over materialism. If we look at successful small cities around the country, those that are vibrant and interesting and sought-after places to live (Cambridge, Georgetown, Greenwich Village), we notice three traits that they share. The first is a high population density, of about 100 units per acre (around ten times the density of most of Davis). This is achieved by a grid system of streets and attached buildings of five or six stories, not so high as to be intimidating, or to create the effect of urban canyons. The second feature is a mixed use zoning, so that the ground floors of the buildings are for businesses, and the upper floors are residential. The third feature is hostility to the automobile. Traffic is slow, parking is difficult to find and extremely expensive. Conversely, public transportation is effective.

The small town mindset rejects all of these notions. Widely-spaced detached single family homes in the rural tradition are considered to be almost the only suitable housing, commercial zoning is scrupulously separated from residential, and the automobile is never offended. An obvious result is urban sprawl. A less obvious result is housing that is unsuited to the needs of a diverse populace. Single family tract housing is best suited to traditional families with children. But there are many non-traditional families, and older couples whose children have left home, and single people, and childless couples who travel a lot, for whom a single-family house is not the best housing. An urban condominium from which one can walk to restaurants and shops, and which relieves one of the burden of maintaining a yard and a car, is more desirable for many people.

If Davis is to grow by twenty thousand people in the next few decades, it would be most appropriate to leave the amount of single-family detached housing at the present level, and put that growth into a dense, vibrant urban core. This would achieve a balance of housing in the city that better suits the needs of a diverse population; it would preserve farmland and open space; and it would create a desirable and economically vital city center. There are substantial technical and economic problems to bringing this about, but they are soluble, provided that there is first of all a clear vision of what it is one hopes to achieve.

There is another way to create high density housing, and that is to build a series of isolated, tall, residential towers. In the architect's sketch the tower is shown arising from a meadow, but in reality it is usually sited in the midst of a vast, windy parking lot. This was Le Corbusier's vision. It has been built many times around the world, and it is almost always a failure. The archipelago of monoliths can force a lot of dwelling units to the acre, but it is not a city, and the urban virtues do not thrive there.

Figure 64. Stevenson Bridge (1923).

Chapter Eleven:

Wealth is Theft

Wealth is theft
Graffito on Stevenson Bridge, 1999

Of the half dozen bridges spanning Putah Creek downstream from Winters, Stevenson Bridge is by far the handsomest. It was built in 1923 to replace a rickety older bridge a hundred yards further east. On the Yolo County side the connecting road was realigned to the new bridge, but on the Solano County side the old road was kept; it runs for miles straight north to the abutment of the abandoned bridge, and at the last moment before plunging into the ravine it makes a right angle turn to the west, and a hundred yards upstream another right angle turn onto the new bridge.

For its first forty years Stevenson Bridge was undecorated. But in 1963 a senior graduating from Dixon High School, much impressed with himself for this achievement, painted his name in large letters on the bridge. This started a tradition of painting graffiti on the bridge, and the bridge has become a sort of public bulletin board. Most of the graffiti are boasts of athletic prowess, or declarations of eternal love (or their more urgent and explicit variations). But sometimes political or philosophical messages appear as well. And so I was not surprised to find one morning a new graffito on the bridge (in gold paint, no less) proclaiming, 'Wealth is theft.'

The aphorism 'wealth is theft' is open to so many interpretations that a room full of professors could discuss it for a year without reaching any consensus. And yet my immediate reaction to it was one of agreement—it struck me as containing a fundamental truth despite its vagueness. In this chapter I offer three brief meditations on, 'wealth is theft,' which relate in a round about way to the landscape.

VALUE OF LABOR

A rather simple-minded Marxist interpretation of 'wealth is theft' might proceed from the notion that value is created by human labor. When an individual has accumulated wealth exceeding his own labor, then he must have done so by expropriating the labor of others. Although we now recognize that there are many sources of value, and may roads to wealth, this formulation is nonetheless valid. The wealth of the farming country in the district is built on human labor, and in general the wealth has not gone to those who have worked the hardest.

Two generations ago, most of the work on farms, with the exception of tillage, was hand labor. It was common to see crews of a few dozen men hoeing the weeds out of an eighty acre field.

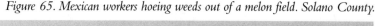

Figure 65. Mexican workers hoeing weeds out of a melon field. Solano County.

Pruning, planting, and irrigation required a large amount of hand labor. Nuts were harvested by banging the branches of the tree with bamboo poles, or hitting the trunk with a huge rubber mallet, and then raking up the fallen nuts by hand. The harvest of apricots and plums and peaches was by hand picking, and there was much post-harvest labor as well, in the packing of the fruit, or in cutting and pitting it and setting the halves on trays in the sun to dry. Tomato harvest required as much as a hundred men (and sometimes a few women) in the field, on their knees, gathering the fruit into wooden lug boxes. Other workers stacked the boxes onto flatbed trucks for their journey to the cannery.

In general, the owner of the farm was not to be found among the laborers in the fields. This is not to say that the farmer was not a hard worker. But he was more likely to be driving a tractor, or maintaining equipment and buildings, or purchasing, or arranging credit, or making sales, or directing the foremen who managed the crews. It would be rare to find him with a hoe in his hand. So early on there developed a two-tiered class system: farmer, and farm-worker. And in agriculture as in industry, the worker was poorly compensated for his labor, and the farmer accrued wealth accordingly.

Who were the workers? In the nineteenth century many were Chinese. There had been a large Chinese presence in California even prior to statehood, and many more were enticed to immigrate by the gold rush, or were recruited to work on the railroads. But if California needed Chinese workers, it also feared them, and a series of powerful anti-Asian racist laws were passed in California, culminating in the Alien Land Act of 1913, which prohibited most Asians from owning land, (and which was not found unconstitutional until 1952!). In addition to doing hired work on farms, a few Chinese leased plots of land in the district and raised most of the fresh produce for local markets.

In the twentieth century many Filipino and Japanese farm workers made their way to the district. By 1940, the population of Winters was more than 15% Japanese, and the Japanese farmers were known for their meticulously kept farms. But early in World War II the Japanese were rounded up and sent to internment camps, and few returned after the war. Like the Chinese, most did not own their farms, and ugly anti-Japanese incidents in Winters, including burning of the Japanese Buddhist temple, deterred most from returning.

It is difficult to evaluate the effect on the landscape of those anti-Asian practices that kept Japanese and Chinese from owning farms in the district. In studying a landscape one must not only see what is there, but also imagine what might have been there, but is not. It is likely that the district has suffered architectural impoverishment as a result of denying land ownership to Asians. And the opportunity for some appealing unorthodoxies in the laying out of a farm has also been lost.

In the 1930's another group of itinerant laborers began working in the district. These were immigrants from the dust bowl states. The remains of an old Okie/Arkie settlement persist on Meridian Road in Solano County—small parcels of land with run down houses, gridlocks of rusting, abandoned cars, and in the back slowly collapsing chicken coops from what had once been a small poultry industry. With the onset of World War II, most of the Okies left farm work for high-paying jobs in the booming war industries. This coincided with the exodus of Japanese to the labor camps, and of many local young men into the armed forces, resulting in a severe labor shortage. Housewives and school children worked in the orchards during the war.

Since 1946, Mexico, especially the states of Jalisco and Michoacan, has been the primary source of farm workers for the region. Their numbers are fewer than once they were, because of the mechanization of harvesting, and because increased use of herbicides has decreased the need for hand weeding. But there is still plenty of labor to be done—pruning, irrigating, transplanting, and operating machinery. It used to be that Mexican farm-workers walking along the roadside were a constant feature of the rural scene. Now they have cars, and have become invisible.

One could say that democracy has made progress in the twentieth century. Land ownership is now open to anyone who has the money, and we find farmers in the district whose origins are Chinese, Japanese, Greek, Italian, Anglo, Pakistani, Mexican, and Hmong. But if the upper tier is democratic, the bottom tier is very solidly made up of dark-skinned people—mostly Mexican, and a few Southeast Asians. There are only a couple of white farm workers in the district and no black farm workers or farmers, the black people of this region being strictly urban. Even when unemployment has been high, white people do not wish to do farm labor. This is a mystery to me, for it is a very satisfying kind of work. But minimum wage with no benefits is probably a deterrent; perhaps the worker recognizes that much of the value of his labor will accrue to the landowner. In the meantime, Mexico is poor, and many desperate souls are happy to have work. In the last half century, the wealth of California agriculture has been built on the poverty of Mexico.

SPENDING OUR CHILDREN'S INHERITANCE

I know of an attorney married to a real estate broker. They own an airplane, a boat, snowmobiles, jet skis, and three cars, which do not fit in the three-car garage of their four-thousand-square-foot house because the garage is full of possessions. They keep the house heated or cooled year round even if they are out of town for a week, and their gas and electric meters are always running. The maid has been instructed to dry the laundry in an electric clothes dryer—they do not have a clothes line in the yard. When they retire in a few years it would not surprise me if they buy an enormous motor home and take a tour around the country, a thing such people seem to do. Perhaps on the back bumper of the motor home they will put a sticker that says, 'We are spending our children's inheritance.' The bumper sticker is only half a jest.

I cannot fathom any sort of balance between the meager contribution these people make to society and the large amount of goods and services they consume. If we accept that the world's resources are limited, then an individual taking a disproportionate share does so at the expense of someone else, perhaps someone not yet born. That their house is twice as big as need be means that a bit more forest has been clear cut, that a bit more fossil fuel has been burned in manufacturing glass and tile and pipe, that the air is a bit dirtier, that there is an increment more traffic on the road to serve the maintenance needs of the house.

The compulsion to acquire goods seems a pathology in our relationship to the material world. And yet the word 'pathology' isn't quite right, for the trait is nearly universal. Cultures that we admire for their moderation in acquiring possessions usually are expressing a lack of means rather than a lack of will. But if it is not pathology, it is at least immaturity, a stage of development one might pass through to arrive at a more enlightened relationship. Some achieve wisdom early; others never get there.

Once I overheard a conversation in which someone not present was being ridiculed for his habit of straightening and reusing bent nails. I do not know the person discussed, and so I can only guess his motives; the speakers supposed it was a question of being extraordinarily cheap, or to put a more positive spin on it, thrifty. Thriftiness is typified by a caricature Scotsman, who straightens bent nails to save a few pennies, and also to gain moral credits by avoiding waste. One imagines God peering over the edge of a cloud at the nail-straightener, and then taking a quill pen and writing in a big book: 'Aug. 6. Angus MacTavish, straighten 3 doz. bnt. Nails. Good wrk.' However, there are good reasons to straighten a nail other than thrift, and without regard to a few pennies one way or the other. A nail has intrinsic value. It is the culmination of forty centuries of metallurgy, and it represents much human ingenuity. Iron with the oxygen driven from it, melded with a few other metals (tungsten, nickel perhaps) is exceptional on our planet, and goes against the grain of planetary chemistry, which would oxidize it back to rust soon enough. Even the oldest square nails of the district were machine made, but with a hard-working operator running the press, and plenty of hard labor spent in filling a wooden nail keg and loading it on a train for the journey to California. The nail deserves respect, for itself, and for the people who made it. I can imagine the nail straightener to be one who has forged a thoughtful relationship to the material world, one based on an ethic of respect. At least, having the leisure to straighten bent nails is the sign of an unhurried life—one that is not devoted to scampering after wealth.

The problem, of course, is not with wealth, but with how it is used. Some people become wealthy unintentionally, by patenting a useful device, or by recording a haunting piece of music, or by simply failing to spend what they are allotted. And when such a person lives moderately, then the wealth is unneeded at home and can be used properly, that is, in support of the arts, and conservation, and education, and charity. Wealth used in this way becomes public wealth—it enriches the community. The parks, concert halls, museums, gardens, and schools are the true wealth of the community, not the Porsche kept under wraps in a rich man's heated garage.

In the landscape of the Putah Creek alluvial fan, conspicuous displays of wealth are uncommon. True, there are some needlessly large and ostentatious houses in town, and even the average is far above modest, but real extravagance is rare. It is not that there are few wealthy people, but lack of restraint is held to be in poor taste—perhaps this represents some maturation of the public perception of materialism. I suspect also that most of those who are old enough to have acquired considerable wealth are wise enough to see the value of simplicity. Maybe they even straighten bent nails. And conversely, the public wealth of the region is great, and its worthy institutions are well supported. These bland remarks acquire some force if we compare Putah Creek to the next valley westward, just over the hill: the Napa Valley. In the Napa valley the culture of wealth and materialism is different, and ostentation bears no onus. And so we find extravagantly wasteful buildings, and a landscape of architectural follies that seems like a bad dream of Disneyland. All that misused material, all that misspent energy, can be reckoned a sort of theft.

RURAL GENTRY

A real estate developer buys a forty acre plot of farm land on the edge of town for $200,000, and holds it for ten years waiting the opportunity to develop it. Finally he gets his permits. He spends six million dollars on engineering—grading, paving, sewers, utilities. The land is subdivided into five lots per acre, for a total of two hundred lots. The lots are sold at $130,000 each, and after deducting his costs the developer walks off with twenty million dollars in his pocket. This is what motivates a developer—to make his twenty million and clear out.

The profit is so out of proportion to the performance that it can only be considered an act of theft. Even the most brazen capitalist should blush. But if it is theft, who are the victims? The most obvious are those who have paid inflated prices for their houses. Somewhat less obvious are those who are shut out of the housing market altogether because these extravagant houses will never be within their means. (Consider for a moment, an alternative path of development. A not-for-profit agency develops the land and sells lots at cost—$30-40,000. The land then is accessible to the farm worker with four

Figure 66. The suburbanesque rural houses of urban refugees. Yolo County

children, the single parent, the artist who wishes to build a studio and small house, the retired person on a limited pension) But the most insidious consequence of this type of urban development occurs in the rural countryside.

When a tenth-of-an-acre lot in town sells for nearly the same price as a forty acre plot of farmland a few miles out of town, many buyers looking for a home site will chose the farmland. The value of a piece of rural land has three components: its value as a producer of farm commodities, its speculative value, and its value as a home site. With the agricultural economy deeply depressed, the farm value of rural land is very low compared to its speculative value and its value as a place to build a house. And so farm land is being sold as forty-acre building lots. I saw an advertisement recently for a plot of rural land; it read: 'Ninety-acre home site, secluded, great views, easy commute.' No mention was made of the farming potential of the land. Is it rice ground or orchard ground? Does it have district water or its own wells? Its value as a place to build a house has eclipsed its agricultural value.

In the last ten years the majority of farmland sold in the district has been sold to non-farmers. Doctors, professors, lawyers, engineers, and businessmen are the new owners. They have no interest in farming; they just want a place to build a big house unrestrained by the tight regulation of city building, and perhaps to add a tennis court and a pool and a barn with a couple of horses. They expect that some tenant farmer will be interested in farming the remainder of the land, and usually they can find someone. Typically it is the biggest corporate farms that are interested in picking up such leases.

The consequences for the landscape are two-fold. First, many large, suburbanesque houses are being built throughout the rural district. They are obviously not working farmsteads; and there is something fraudulent about them. The second consequence is that the land is farmed by tenant farmers, typically corporations that embody the practices of industrial farming, that is, farming for short-term dollars rather than for long-term enrichment of the land.

There is a phenomenon we might call 'the paradox of rurality.' It is a cousin to the paradox of wilderness, which goes like this. We value wilderness for the absence of humans and their artifacts; by setting foot in the wilderness, we contaminate it and lessen it. The dream of wilderness is more pure than the wilderness itself, which is disturbed by our presence. Surely, Yosemite valley with fifty thousand tourists in it is not a wild place. Similarly, people are attracted to the rural countryside by the deep beauty of its landscape, by its orderliness, by the abundance of its fields and the prosperity of its orchards, and by the purposefulness of its workers. But when the urbanite builds a country house, he has sure enough begun to ruin the countryside that attracted him. For he has no real business being there, his house is non-organic to the landscape, and when dozens of such houses are scattered through the countryside, the rural district loses its authenticity. It becomes a diluted suburbia.

When the wealthy townsman builds his place in the country, he inadvertently harms the young man or young woman who has few assets and who wishes to become a farmer. What is this person to do? When a parcel of rural land has been encumbered with a $600,000 house, no would-be farmer can afford it. The extravagant house has alienated the farmland from the farmer. The best bet for this person is to arrange a lease of land owned by a rural urbanite. So the farmer lives in town, and commutes to his fields, and on the road he passes the rich doctor who owns the land, and lives on the farm, and commutes to his office in town. This is not a good situation. To farm well, one must follow practices that are unprofitable in the short term, but that enhance the health of the land in the long term. It would take an unusual degree of wisdom for the young farmer to farm well on land that he does not own simply because it is the righteous thing to do. One could not blame him for cutting some corners, and farming badly, if he has no assurance that he will be there a year from now.

In Scandinavia, where good farmland is scarce, the sale of farmland is regulated by government. The purchaser must be a genuine farmer, not just someone with a lot of money and a wish for a country place. Regrettably, such regulation would not be feasible here because of the exaggerated notion of personal freedom engrained in our culture. A Farmlands Commission, with powers analogous to those of the Coastal Commission or the commissions that oversee historic districts, is badly needed.

In some instances, the urban professionals buying rural property in the district may be better stewards of their land than the farmer that owned it before them. Many of the new owners are knowledgeable about ecology and about the ethics of stewardship, and have abundant financial resources. Ideally, these owners could form a long-term alliance with a young farmer, with a durable lease that protects the owners and yet gives the farmer enough security that he is motivated to farm the land as if it were his own.

Figure 67. Almond orchard. Solano County

Chapter Twelve:

The Experience of Landscape

> We shall not cease from exploration
> And the end of all our exploring
> Will be to arrive where we started
> And know the place for the first time.
> T.S. Eliot, *Four Quartets*

THE LANDSCAPE AS IMAGE

The word 'landscape' entered English 500 years ago from Dutch, where it was applied to a class of paintings in which the human figure was of small significance compared to a view of countryside. This use of the word persists, and influences our thinking. A painting of a landscape has these salient features: there is no motion in the scene; among the sense it appeals only to vision; there is a frame around it; and because of perspective used by the painter, the viewer is placed outside of the scene rather than within it. It is well known and oft repeated how the 18th century English garden designers attempted to create real landscapes that mimic landscape paintings, particularly those of Claude Lorraine and Nicolas Poussin. The paths in these gardens connected a series of vantage points where one might stand and survey the scene. The similarities of these views to a painting are several: the view may be framed (by foliage); the viewer is still, so that there is no motion; and the scene is distant so that the viewer is outside of it rather than within it. In modern times, the highway department continues this notion of the picturesque landscape. The road sign indicates a scenic viewpoint ahead, and the motorists dutifully pull off. The scene is experienced through the viewfinder of a camera, which renders it static and purely visual, puts a frame around it, and removes the viewer from the scene. This is a voyeuristic relationship to the landscape, in which landscape is reduced to mere scenery.

    The modern traveler usually sees a landscape from an automobile. The scene has a frame around it—the windshield frame of the car, perhaps interrupted by a rearview mirror and a parking sticker in one corner. If he wears eyeglasses, these also put a frame around the scene. The

> It is impossible for material order to exist side by side with spiritual disorder.
> Wendell Berry, *The Body and the Earth*

motorist is isolated from the sounds and smells of the landscape, and experiences it only in visual terms. If he is taken with a view, he may stop and photograph it, preserving it in the picturesque mode.

The motorist encapsulated in his automobile may be only barely attentive to the landscape. If he were to park the car and get out and walk, he would experience the landscape in a more engaging way. All of our senses and our machinery of perception have evolved to operate at the scale and pace of walking through open country. Walking along a paved road, straight and flat, the traveler's attention may wander, and yet unconsciously he is registering the sound of a distant tractor, and the heat of the sun on his cheek, and the sweet smell of star thistle in a sunny pasture. Perhaps the traveler leaves the road and strikes out along a farm trail. The visual scene may be of only passing interest, for the farm country is laid out with such regularity that a single glance suffices to solve the riddle of its pattern. And so the traveler's mind yet may wander, though he must pay more attention to irregularities in the footing on the trail than he did walking on the road. If the traveler now reaches the channel of the creek, and if he leaves the flat farm country and the trail and drops down into the riparian forest where there is no trail, then moving through the landscape will require all of his attention. Should he go over this fallen log or around it? There's some water on the right as well as the left; has he strayed onto a peninsula? Should he backtrack? He studies the scene. Look out for that poison oak over there. There might be an easy passage along that row of willows.

The foot traveler whose path is not on a trail becomes fully engaged with the landscape. He is dealing with landscape as an image, but it is not framed, it is not static, and he is within it rather than outside of it; he moves on the brightly lit stage rather than sitting in the darkened auditorium on the other side of the proscenium.

THE LANDSCAPE AS TEXT

The annotations and captions to the landscape image constitute the landscape as text. In the preceding chapters I have offered some interpretations of images of the Putah Creek alluvial fan. Another person, considering the same landscape, might invent a very different narrative to go with it, and one that is equally valid. And if I were to attempt this reading again a decade hence, I might also produce a very different narrative. The deep text of the landscape includes readings by many people at many times. Better yet, if we could fathom them, would be readings by hawk, dragonfly, mouse, skunk, and valley oak.

We speak of 'reading the landscape,' by which we mean drawing meanings from it, which is the public and universal side of the text, but we could also speak of 'writing the landscape,' projecting meanings into it, which is a personal and private dimension of the text. There is no single, linear text, but many texts running simultaneously: an aesthetic narrative, an ecological narrative, and economic narrative, and many others.

One could make a musical analogy. To the young person noticing a landscape for the first time, the experience is like a clear melody played on a solo clarinet (for some it's a solo kazoo). To a slightly older viewer the text of the landscape is an allegro played by a quintet—the clarinet is joined in a witty conversation by other friendly voices. To the yet older and more experienced person who comprehends simultaneously many texts, the scene is more heavily orchestrated—a symphony. Some will be very analytical about it, and insist on distinguishing the notes of the oboe from those of the clarinet, but the complex sound can also be experienced as a whole without the need to dissect its various parts. If the listener is familiar with the work, then his experience is overlain with memory and anticipation—the hushed reverberations of previous performances. To one even older, the symphony of text is being played from a very worn vinyl LP; there is a lot of static, and scratches, and inexplicably missing passages, and fragments that repeat endlessly until someone jiggles the needle. If a sad memory is associated with a landscape image, then the score may be modulated to a minor key. These comments apply to an observer of the landscape who is alert and attentive; there will be some for whom the experience never progresses beyond three notes on a kazoo.

COHERENCE OF THE RURAL LANDSCAPE

Imagine the rural landscape of the district in 1940, a time at which it was most coherent. The foot traveler walking from Davis to Winters would pass several dozen farms, all similar, but none the same. There would be variations in the ornamentation and spacing and construction of buildings; and in the apportioning of land among pasture, field, and orchard; and in the placement of fences

Figure 68. Sunflowers. Solano County

and ditches. The farms would be variations on a theme, and their composition would be governed by an unwritten set of rules. The traveler who apprehended the poetics of the landscape would find it congenial and consistent.

If we try to discover what those unwritten rules were by which the landscape was ordered, perhaps the first to emerge would be the primacy of the straight line. In flat country, the straight line is the line of most efficient motion. Animals travel in a sequence of straight lines, from cover to cover, or prospect to prospect, or grazing spot to grazing spot. Straight lines simplify surveying, and the making of maps and laying out of parcels, and the setting out of fences, and the management of land. And for tillage and cultivation, a straight line is most efficient. Neither a team nor a tractor works efficiently through a curve. A harrow which is ten feet wide, for example, as it goes through a curve addresses the line of travel at an angle, so that it harrows less than ten feet of width, and a curving path results in strips of uneven width, which complicates tillage and cultivation. So the landscape of the district is ordered by straight lines. In contrast, in mountainous country curved and irregular lines are most appropriate, and straight lines impractical.

In the buildings of the rural countryside, too, one finds a conventionality which consists of a collection of mild constraints rather than a forced conformity such as one might find in buildings constructed by a government. One learns to expect a certain relationship of house, barn, tank tower, and windmill; a certain pattern of paths and fences and gates; a certain style of dooryard plantings. The houses are raised above the ground, rather than set into it, and they are outward-looking, with windows on all sides. There are no astounding surprises to be encountered on this walk.

Except for dividing a portion of the district into township and range, the coherence of the landscape was achieved without a master plan. No individual, nor any committee, made formal decisions about how the landscape was to be ordered, or farms laid out, or buildings erected, and yet the result was very consistent. In part this is due to the shared culture of the farmers. Although they came from many nations, they learned mostly from each other (as they still do), and imitation, with variations, of successful farms was the origin of many conventions and idioms of land use. It is also true that the situational logic of the district's ecology provided an envelope of constraints. In country without stone, one does not build a stone house. If there is only one tank tower builder in the district, you will get the kind of tank tower that he knows how to build, and not some other.

Throughout the world, landscapes that have been created under a set of constraints, and which thereby achieve a degree of coherence, are attractive. The traveler discerns the pattern, and then can appreciate the subtle variations that have been wrought within the set limits. More severe constraints often make more appealing landscapes—think of the outer Hebrides, or the Greek Islands, or the high valleys of Tibet. Human ingenuity thrives when it is well hedged in. Less happy is the landscape deliberately created by a planning authority with its own set of rules, often arbitrary. Such a landscape is likely to have repetitions of identical structures. What is most congenial to the human mind is not identical reiterations, but subtle variations on a theme. Our ancestors evolved in an environment where it was critical to distinguish one human from another, friend from foe, and edible plant from poisonous plant. And so much of our neural architecture is devoted to an appreciation of family resemblances in relation to individual differences. We are predisposed to become taxonomists. We find a museum case of related beetles, or an album of family photos, to be endlessly interesting as we sort out individuality and familiality. This ability is innate with us, and underlies our appreciation of a coherent landscape.

In the period since 1940 the coherence of the landscape in the district has eroded. Many people now live in the countryside who are not farmers, and the harmony of purpose of the old population is lost. And constraints have been loosened because there is too much wealth, and commerce has been made too easy. The rich lawyer who buys rural land in the district to build a house can build in any style he chooses. There are no limits. And there is a spate of architects eager to flaunt their cleverness and outrageousness. A slate roof imported from China? Why not? (There is one such roof in the district now). But the obverse of creative freedom in building is regional architectural incoherence. The poetics of the landscape unravel, and visual chaos ensues. We can see this in the Napa Valley, where the innate beauty of the place is marred by incoherent building. This is the unwholesome shadow of too much wealth, too much freedom, and too much ostentatious individuality, and it seems to be ever increasing in the district of Putah Creek.

FRAMES OF REFERENCE

If you ask a town person for directions, he will say, 'Go to the next intersection and turn to your right.' If you ask a country person for directions, he will say, 'Go to the next intersection and turn to the north.' The difference is revealing.

The town dweller, deprived of a vista by the spurious curvature of suburban streets, and denied the horizon by buildings and vegetation, has no view. He hardly considers the progression of the sun across the sky, and is unacquainted with the moon. Without landmarks, he takes a self-centered point of reference, places the zero of abscissa and ordinate in the center of his own head, and says, 'Turn to the right.'

The farmer, standing in his field a few miles west of town, has a broad view. Twenty miles to the west he sees the crest of the coast range, his gaze anchored by the deep 'V' of the Berryessa notch. Seventy miles to the north he can make out the Sutter Buttes, an ancient volcanic cone, and a compass point and a half eastward of that is the snowy triangle of Mt. Lassen, one hundred twenty miles distant. Due east is the crest of the Sierra Nevada, ninety miles off, and south by seventy miles sits Mt. Diablo, with its double hump. The country person follows the daily passage of the sun, and its retreat to the south in winter, and northward migration in spring. If he steps outside at midnight and sees a rising half moon, he knows without pondering it that this is a waning moon and not a waxing one. He is familiar with the rotation of the stars, and reckons the hour by the position of Orion.

The country person imagines himself and his fellows moving about on this spacious stage from a perspective somewhere overhead. It is a hawk's-eye view of the land. It is the view that God had before airplanes were invented. And so he says, 'Turn to the north.'

THE HUMAN FIGURE IN THE LANDSCAPE

The average population density of the Putah Creek alluvial fan is more than five hundred people per square mile. And yet, once you have left the borders of town, there are few people to be seen. Indeed, the countryside is much less populous than it was fifty years ago, for machines now do farm work that used to be done by humans.

An occasional car may speed by, but traffic on the county roads is sparse. More commonly one sees bicycles. Some I think of as bicyclists from Mars. They wear bizarre costumes of stretchy, shiny material, and pod-like helmets strapped to their heads. Mostly they travel in tight packs at high speed. They seem to be aliens in the landscape, on tour from outer space, and probably one

Figure 69. Hmong strawberry workers. Yolo County

such returns from his thirty mile ride having seen nothing more than the rear wheel of the bicycle that is six inches in front of him. Other cyclists are more human. Once, far from town, I came across an old Chinese man riding a battered bike at about three miles per hour. He was steering with one hand and holding a cigarette with the other, looking happily about at the orchards through which he passed.

In the countryside, people on foot are rare. Near town one encounters joggers. Like the bicyclists from Mars, they seem self-preoccupied and disengaged from the landscape. I saw one old fellow stop and consult the dial of a device strapped to his arm, perhaps to verify that his heart was beating, since he had forgotten the more direct way of figuring it. Occasionally you will see a farm worker tending irrigation— standing in a muddy field, or walking along a ditch with a shovel over his shoulder, or carrying an armload of aluminum siphons. Rarest of all, you will find people simply walking, perhaps with a destination, perhaps not. This mystifies me. Walking is a fundamental human activity—it is what the last million years of our evolution have made us good at. Walking is a tonic to the mind and spirit and body. And it gets you where you need to go. I am the only one in my neighborhood who walks to town, which is only six miles, and doesn't take long. The rest require a ton and a half of steel to get themselves there.

A MODEST PROPOSAL

Here is a modest proposal: that all of the inhabitants of the region share a Sabbath. The airplanes will be left in their hangars, the tractors in their sheds, the cars and motorcycles parked wherever they might be. No machinery will be operated, no lawnmowers or leaf blowers or chain saws. Fans and compressors and other electric devices will be shut down. The lights will be extinguished, with no hum of fluorescent tubes. Computers, too, will be extinguished. Guns will not be fired. Radios and CD players and televisions will be silenced. Stores will be closed. Commerce will cease. People will refrain from work. All will be at leisure. They might visit with family and friends, walk in gardens or parks or out into the countryside, perhaps take a picnic. Some might sing.

The term Sabbath is meant here not in a religious sense, but in a spiritual one. Never has there been a culture so hostile to the realm of spirit as our own. The triumph of materialism has been achieved with a corresponding denigration of spirit. The area in which we come closest to the world of spirit is in music—the most nearly blameless of human achievements. And the appalling state of the soundscape indicates our low regard for spirit. Engines, sirens, gunfire, and barking dogs are the dominant sound of the region. Local churches—a jumble of mismatched buildings with locked doors—seem a poor sort of place for an attitude of reverence. Their justification is that they can partly shelter their inhabitants from the noise outside. Perhaps the most astonishing feature of a true Sabbath would be the discovery of how quiet and peaceful the world can be. Many people do not much notice the noise in which they live; it is like a chronic headache that one has got used to. One does not realize how bad it is until, suddenly and astonishingly, it stops.

If such a Sabbath were held even once, people would talk about for the rest of their lives. If it were held once a year, it would be the high point of the year. And if it occurred once a week, we would all be better people. And yet, what is proposed is nothing more than the birthright of all humans, the basic condition of the human world for the last ten thousand years excepting the most recent century. To the extent that the proposal seems preposterous, it is a measure of our alienation.

WALKING HOME FROM THE LIBRARY

I step out the door of the University Library in the late afternoon. The campus is lovely, park-like, a landscape untainted by commerce, or automobiles. The electric and phone wires are underground, removing a visual annoyance. And the presence of intelligent and idealistic young people (some of them, anyway) is hopeful. I have six miles to go, and I set off at a good pace. Already the Delta breeze is blowing, whispering a message from the sea. Leaving the center and moving to the periphery of the campus the level of formality diminishes; the grounds are less well kept and

Figure 70. Putah Creek

wilder, the people fewer. I pass dairy barns, a highway, sheep barns. The road I follow heads southwest until it reaches the creek.

Putah Creek, the shy protagonist of this narrative, is seldom seen. The creek runs in the bottom of a deep arroyo, hidden by dense riparian forest of willows, cottonwoods, box elders, walnuts, and oaks. The creek channel cannot be seen from a distance; it is only when you are nearly on top of it that you can look down into it. The orderly plane of our existence, the landscape of towns and farms, is at certain level, and the diagonal streak of wildness lies well below it. One leaves civilization behind and descends into the creek channel in a way that one might plumb elements of wildness within one's self.

I walk on a paved road along the northern bank of the creek, looking down into the channel. I recognize a place where I used to play when I was a child. There were three of us who liked to play at being Indians. Who knows where our notion of Indians came from—a confabulation of Algonquin and Mohawk lore? But we knew well enough what it meant. It meant walking with utter silence and stealth, and speaking the languages of animals, and reading invisible signs in rocks and trees. There was another lad who always wanted to be a cowboy—to wear big boots and stomp on things and shoot loud guns. I wonder what became of the other two Indians, and if they found gentle occupations. I know well enough about the cowboy; I'm surrounded by his ilk.

I leave the paved road, which cuts to the north, and continue along the creek on a gravel spur, the creek on one side, plowed fields on the other. At Country Road 98 there is a concrete bridge, and I cross to the Solano County side. From the center of the bridge I can look forty feet down into the shallow water, teeming with fish and cast-off tires. At the far side I squeeze through a hole in a chain-link fence and angle westward on a dirt track. At this season it is dust, except in a few places where an irrigation ditch has failed, and the ground is muddy.

The sound of gunfire becomes audible. The firing range is more than five miles away, at roads 29 and 95, right in the center of the district. A quick mental calculation shows that the sound covers at least 45,000 acres of rural land. When the range first opened, it was used by just an occasional person with a 22. But now the sound is continuous, dawn to dark, seven days a week. And the guns are likely to be AK-47's and Uzis and the big 50 millimeter rifles that can be heard twelve miles away. Gunfire is especially brisk on Sundays; Christians, no doubt, blasting away at a paper target in the shape of a helpless, fleeing man.

I pass corn fields, and a clump of fig trees surviving at an abandoned homestead. In the distance are two concrete silos, indicating that once there was a dairy here, though it is many years gone. The corn ends, and I reach a small field of watermelons. A Mexican man is tending irrigation. I greet him, 'Buenas tardes, Senor, que tal?' We shake hands. He offers me a cigarette. I decline. He lights one for himself. 'Good looking field of melons.' I say. 'Are they being grown for seed, or for eating?'

'For seed,' he says, 'but a few of them manage to get eaten.'

We study the melons. There is no hurry to such a conversation. 'The breeze is strong tonight,' he says. 'It started early.'

'You'll be needing two blankets by dawn.' I observe.

We regard a disorderly stream of crows flying from the southwest.

After a bit I bid him farewell and continue on my way. It is a curious thing that the word 'civility' comes from a root meaning 'city,' and yet it is not in the city, but in the remotest parts of the countryside that people are most civil. In town you cannot stop and greet every person you meet; you would never reach your destination. But in the country an older way persists.

The sky-diving plane is passing overhead—its fifth circuit since I started walking. It is an unattractive plane, flying with its nose up and its tail dragging and the engine at full throttle, so that the heavens reverberate from horizon to horizon, and the ear drums of every living creature in the district are assaulted with noise. And for what? So that some junior attorney from San Francisco can jump out of the plane in the hope of putting a momentary thrill into his meaningless life. If ever there was a civilization that deserved to perish, ours is the one.

The melon field is past; now I'm skirting a field of wheat stubble. I see a jackrabbit coming along the track toward me. We both stop, he stands on his hind feet and regards me with a large and fearful eye. 'Good afternoon, Mr. Long Ears.' I say. Then I step out into the field and let him pass. I see no reason why he should defer to me rather than the other way around.

Back on the path I study animal tracks in the dust at the edge of the creek channel. I make out quail and dove, possum and raccoon, magpie and crow, skunk and fox, mouse and lizard, and the sinuous signature of a snake. Further along I pass a heap of abandoned concrete pipes—

someone's unfulfilled hydraulic dream. A young almond orchard to the south will be ready for its second harvest, with a good crop. I remember when this field was once in beans, and I walked through it on a cloudy afternoon when a shaft of sunlight came through at a low angle, backlighting the beans with a golden aura, etching the scene in my memory. That would have been five or six years ago.

    I cross a road, and reach a stout fence around an orchard of fruit trees. It is a fencing-out fence. It probably cost far more than the value of any fruit that might be pilfered in this out-of-the-way place. The fence represents the urban values of the absentee owners. I jump it, not gracefully, but without injury. A ways further on I climb over a wooden fence into what had been a horse pasture, and is now a field of peppers. At the end of the pepper field I climb over another horse fence. Just ahead is an orchard of citrus, and an avenue of olive trees flanking a narrow dirt road that leads to a small house with a tin roof. Home.

A SENSE OF ORDER

Pertinent Literature

1. Bainer R: Science and technology in Western agriculture, in Shideler, JH (ed): *Agriculture in the Development of the Far West*, The Agricultural History Society, Washington, 1975, pp 56-72.
2. Baker TL: *A Field Guide to American Windmills*, Univ. of Oklahoma Press, Norman, 1985.
3. Barbour M, Major J: *Terrestrial Vegetation of California*, J Wiley & Sons, New York & London, 1977
4. Berry W: *The Unsettling of America: Culture & Agriculture*, Sierra Club Books, San Francisco, 1977
5. Berry W: Whose head is the farmer using? Whose head is using the farmer? in Jackson, W et al. (eds): *Meeting the Expectations of the Land,* North Point Press, San Francisco, 1984
6. Berry W: A Native Hill, in *Recollected Essays*, 1965-1980, North Point Press, San Francisco, 1981
7. Berry W: The Body and the Earth, in *Recollected Essays*, 1965-1980, North Point Press, San Francisco, 1981
8. Bromfield L: *Malabar Farm*, Harper & Bros., New York, 1947
9. Bromfield L: *Out of the Earth*, Harper & Bros., New York, 1948
10. Cather W: *O Pioneers!* 1913, reprint, Quality Paperback Book Club, New York, 1995
11. Demetrecopolou Wintun Songs, *Anthropos* 483, 1935, cited by Heizer & Elasser. The quotation given (in H&E) does not appear in the original reference they cite, nor is their page citation correct (483, rather than 383 as given).
12. Eliot TS: *Four Quartets*, Harcourt, Brace & Co., New York, 1943

13. Fukuoka M: *The Natural Way of Farming*, Japan Publications, Inc., Tokyo, 1985

14. Gifford D: *The Farther Shore: A Natural History of Perception*, Random House, New York, 1990

15. Gombrich EH: *The Sense of Order,* Phaidon Press, London, 1979

16. Groth P and Bressi TW (eds): *Understanding Ordinary Landscapes,* Yale University Press, New Haven & London, 1997

17. Haslam, G: *The Other California*, University of Nevada Press, Reno, 1990

18. Heizer RF and Elsasser AB: *The Natural World of the California Indians*, University of California Press, Berkeley, 1980

19. Hill, M: *California Landscape: Origin and Evolution* University of California Press, Berkeley, 1984

20. Howett, CM: Where the one-eyed man is king: the tyranny of visual and formalist values in evaluating landscapes, in Groth P, and Bressi TW (eds): *Understanding Ordinary Landscapes*, Yale Univ. Press, New Haven and London, 1997, pp.85-98

21. Jackson JB: The need for being versed in country things. *Landscape 1(1):*1-5, 1951

22. Jackson JB: A change of plans. *Landscape* 1(3):18-26, 1952

23. Jackson W, Berry W, Colman B: *Meeting the Expectations of the Land*, North Point Press, San Francisco, 1984

24. Johnson S, Haslam G, Dawson R: *The Great Central Valley: California's Heartland*, University of California Press, Berkeley, 1993

25. King, AD: The Politics of Vision, in Groth P, and Bressi TW (eds): *Understanding Ordinary Landscapes* Yale Univ. Press, New Haven and London, 1997, pp.134-144

26. Larkey JL: *Davisville '68: The History and Heritage of the City of Davis*, Davis Historical and Landmarks Commission, Davis, 1969

27. Larkey JL: *Winters: A Heritage of Horticulture, A Harmony of Purpose*, Yolo County Historical Society, Woodland CA, 1991

28. Levi-Strauss, C: *La Pensee Sauvage*, Libaririe Plon, Paris, 1962

29. Lewis, PF: Axioms for reading the landscape, in Meinig, DW (ed) *The Interpretation of Ordinary Landscapes*, Oxford Univ. Press, NY & Oxford, 1979, pp 11-32

30. Logsdon G: The importance of traditional farming practices for a sustainable modern agriculture, in Jackson, W, et al. (eds) *Meeting the Expectations of the Land*, North Point Press, San Francisco, 1984

31. McClatchie AJ: *Eucalypts Cultivated in the United States*, Government Printing Office, Washington, 1902

32. McPhee J: *Assembling California*, Farar, Straus, & Giroux, New York, 1993

33. Meinig, DW (ed): *The Interpretation of Ordinary Landscapes*, Oxford University Press, New York & Oxford, 1979

34. Preston, WL: *Vanishing Landscapes*, University of California Press, Berkeley, 1981

35. Robins, P: *Bring Farm Edges Back to Life!* Yolo County Resource Conservation District, Woodland, CA 1999.

36. Rybczynski, W: *City Life: Urban Expectations in a New World*, Scribner, New York, 1995

37. Scheuring, AF (ed): *A Guidebook to California Agriculture*, University of California Press, Berkeley, 1983

38. Sloane, E: *American Barns and Covered Bridges*, Wilfred Funk, Inc., New York, 1954

39. Sloane, E: *Our Vanishing Landscape,* Wilfred Funk, Inc., New York, 1955

40. Smil, V: *Energy, Food, Environment*, Clarendon Press, Oxford, 1987

41. Smil, V: *Energies,* MIT Press, Cambridge and London, 1999

42. Spirn AW: *The Language of Landscape* Yale University Press, New Haven and London, 1998

43. Steinbeck, J: *East of Eden,* Viking, New York, 1952

44. Townsend J: Looking for the good life, in *Whole Earth Review*, Fall 1987, p. 94

45. USDA Soil Conservation Service: *Soil Survey of Yolo County, California,* US Government

Printing Office, Washington, 1972

46. Watts, May T: *Reading the Landscape*, MacMillan & Co., New York, 1957

47. Worster D: The shaky ground of sustainability, in Sessions, G (ed), *Deep Ecology for the 21st Century*, Shambala, Boston & London, 1995, 417-427

PERTINENT LITERATURE